PAUL AND MISSION

PAUL AND MISSION

by

LUCIEN LEGRAND, MEP

ORBIS BOOKS

Maryknoll, New York 10545

Founded in 1970, Orbis Books endeavors to publish works that enlighten the mind, nourish the spirit, and challenge the conscience. The publishing arm of the Maryknoll Fathers and Brothers, Orbis seeks to explore the global dimensions of the Christian faith and mission, to invite dialogue with diverse cultures and religious traditions, and to serve the cause of reconciliation and peace. The books published reflect the views of their authors and do not represent the official position of the Maryknoll Society. To learn more about Maryknoll and Orbis Books, please visit our website at www.maryknollsociety.org.

Library of Congress Cataloging-in-Publication Data

Names: Legrand, Lucien, 1927- author.
Title: Paul and mission / Lucien Legrand, MEP.
Other titles: Paul et la mission. English
Description: Maryknoll, NY : Orbis Books, [2023] | Originally published: Paul et la mission. Paris : Médiaspaul, 2021. | Includes bibliographical references and index. | Summary: "Explores themes of mission in the writings of Paul"— Provided by publisher.
Identifiers: LCCN 2022051233 (print) | LCCN 2022051234 (ebook) | ISBN 9781626985162 | ISBN 9781608339785 (epub)
Subjects: LCSH: Paul, the Apostle, Saint—Theology. | Missions—Theory.
Classification: LCC BV2063 .L32513 2023 (print) | LCC BV2063 (ebook) | DDC 266—dc23/eng/20230117
LC record available at https://lccn.loc.gov/2022051233
LC ebook record available at https://lccn.loc.gov/2022051234

Contents

Part Two
The Mission

Abbreviations

ACFEB	Association Catholique Française d'Études Bibliques
BETL	Bibliotheca ephemeridum theologicarum lovaniensium
JB	Jerusalem Bible
BP	Benedictina Publishing
BZNW	Beihefte zur Zeitschrift zum neutestamentliche Wissenschaft
CBET	Contributions to Biblical Exegesis and Theology
CBNT	Commentaire Biblique: Nouveau Testament
CC	Continental Commentaries
CNT	Commentaire du Nouveau Testament
DACL	*Dictionnaire d'archéologie chrétienne et de liturgie*
DBT	*Dictionary of Biblical Theology*
EB	Études bibliques
EDNT	*Exegetical Dictionary of the New Testament*
ESV	English Standard Version
ET	*Expository Times*
FRLANT	Forschungen zur Religion und Literatur des Alten und Neuen Testaments
GNT	The Greek New Testament
HNTC	Harper's New Testament Commentaries
HTR	*Harvard Theological Review*
ICC	International Critical Commentary
ITS	*Indian Theological Studies*
JSNT	*Journal for Study of the New Testament*

KEK	Kritisch-exegetischer Kommentar über das Neue Testament
LD	Lectio Divina
LDCom	Lectio Divina Commentaires
NAB	New American Bible
NICNT	New International Commentaries to the New Testament
NIDB	*New Interpreter's Dictionary of the Bible*
NIV	New International Version
NJB	New Jerusalem Bible
NLT	New Living Translation
NRSV	New Revised Standard Version
NTS	*New Testament Studies*
OBO	Orbis Biblicus et Orientalis
RNT	Regensburger Neues Testament
RSPT	*Revue de sciences philosophiques et théologiques*
SBLSBS	Society of Biblical Literature: Sources for Biblical Studies
SBT	Studies in Biblical Theology
SBLit	Studies in Biblical Literature
SNTSMS	Society for New Testament Studies Monograph Series
TDNT	*Theological Dictionary of the New Testament*
TDOT	*Theological Dictionary of the Old Testament*
TLNT	*Theological Lexicon of the New Testament*
VJTR	*Vidyajyothi Journal of Theological Reflections*
WUNT	Wissenschaftliche Untersuchungen zum Neuen Testament

Preface

The COVID-19 pandemic has afforded me the time to engage questions of Paul's mission thought and praxis in new ways. Since this book was first written in French and at the request of a French publisher, the bibliographical notes give preference to French publications. During that time, travel limitations kept me away from India. Yet the insights developed in the book matured in lectures, courses, and publications given mostly in India. They are much indebted also to the vibrant sharing that took place in Indian Biblical and Theological Associations and at the National Biblical Catechetical and Liturgical Centre of Bangalore. They owe much also to the challenge of a ministry in both urban and rural milieu. They owe much to this setting. It is this mission context which determined the topic itself and the need to look at the Apostle from a mission perspective. Much has been written about St. Paul. Rows of our theological libraries cover the various aspects of Paul's views on God, Christ, the church, and Christian life. But, apart from hagiographic and spiritual publications, proportionately little has been done on what could be called Pauline missiology.[1]

---

1. See, however, J. C. Beker, *Paul the Apostle: The Triumph of God in Life and Thought* (Philadelphia: Fortress, 1980); W. A. Meeks, *The First Urban Christians: The Social World of the Apostle Paul* (New Haven: Yale University Press, 1983); D. Senior and C. Stuhlmuller, *Biblical Foundations for Missions* (London: SCM, 1983); E. P. Sanders, *Paul* (Oxford: Oxford University Press, 1991); A. Le Grys, *Preaching to the Nations: The Origins of Mission in the Early Church* (London: SPCK, 1998); Peter Bolt and Mark Thompson (eds.), *The Gospel to the Nations: Perspectives on Paul's Mission* (Leicester: Intervarsity, 2000); L. J. Lietaert Peerbolte, *Paul the Missionary* (Leuven: Peeters, 2003).

At the outset, a preliminary question arises. Was Paul a "missionary" at all? The answer seems to be obvious when we read the Acts of the Apostles. A historian of Christian origins describes in enthusiastic terms the "unbelievable story" of "a soldier of Christ, a fighter for the Good News. . . . Continually on the move, he preaches, argues, convinces. . . . In 20 years how much success and how few failures."[2] But the letters of the Apostle himself are less boastful. They acknowledge failures to the point of evoking the tears of the frustrated evangelizer (2 Cor. 2:4). They lay bare the "weaknesses" of one who "is not worthy to be called an apostle" (1 Cor. 15:9). Judging by the letters of Paul himself, a recent biographer of Paul went to the opposite extent of denying that Paul was a missionary: "The number of kilometers should not obnubilate us. . . . Paul wrote more than he visited. . . . He was not a man of the field. . . . He did not burn with the desire to go on farther ahead. He did not launch into the Christian adventure. He followed ways already well laid out by others."[3]

This may be going too far. If the mileage covered may not be the heart of the matter, the spirit that moved the Apostle cannot be gainsaid. The autobiographic asides given in 2 Corinthians 6:4–10 and 11:23–28 evoke adventurous ways. They are not the language of an armchair theologian.

So, was Paul a missionary and, if so, in which sense? Looking for an answer, we must make sure that the language we use is adequate. In the Indian context particularly, the word "missionary" is fraught with ambiguity. On the one hand, government officials are exhorted to put "missionary zeal" in the accomplishment of their responsibilities, which is an underhanded tribute to the selfless commitment of "missionaries." On the other hand, in Hindutva propaganda, "missionary" connotes a survival of colonialism, aggressive and destructive of Indian culture. Missionaries are supposed to have one aim in mind, "making conver-

---

2. H. Daniel-Rops, *Apôtres et martyrs* (Paris: Fayard, 1965), 64–65.
3. M. F. Baslez, *Saint Paul* (Paris: Fayard, 2012), 331–32.

sions," which are presumed to be "forced conversions," obtained by fraudulent means.

Evidently the Apostle was not that kind of "missionary." He did not represent any foreign influence and showed less concern for statistical importance than for authenticity of faith and love in the community he founded. So, we must look at Paul the Apostle without projecting on him ready-made clichés. In this study, priority must be given to what he says himself of his sense of mission. In the Acts of the Apostles, Luke traces the brilliant picture of an ardent missionary. But this is already an interpretation inspired by one or two generations of post-Pauline spread of the gospel in the Roman Empire. It is so also with the Pastoral Epistles. Therefore, we shall focus our study on the letters that are generally recognized as coming directly from the hand of Paul: Romans, 1–2 Corinthians, Galatians, Philippians, 1 Thessalonians, and Philemon. They are also the most vibrant expression of his apostolic commitment. The Pastoral Epistles (1–2 Timothy, Titus) and the Acts of the Apostles continue to reflect the spirit of the Apostle to the Gentiles, but they adapt it to the new situations that had developed one or two generations afterward.

We are now many generations after Paul, and the present millennium moves at a stunning pace. It makes it even more urgent to base our faith and action on the solid "foundation which is Jesus Christ" (1 Cor. 3:11). This is what Paul did, at the origin of the Christian mission. His guidance will lead us into a deeper understanding of the fundamentals of the mission.

PRELUDE

1

"A Chosen Instrument"

"A chosen instrument": this is how Paul is introduced at the beginning of his ministry in Acts 9:15. Indeed, young Saul was endowed with outstanding human qualities when he met the Risen Lord on the way to Damascus. They were the fruits of a complex socio-economic background.

The Milieu

Tarsus of Cilicia

Tarsus, where he was born, was a fairly important city in the northeastern corner of the Mediterranean Sea. Situated on the border between Asia Minor, facing the West, and Syria, turned toward the East, it was a transit point for trade between Asia and Europe. It was the capital of the rich province of Cilicia, well watered by rivers flowing from the Anatolian highland. Its population of one hundred thousand made it one of the most populous cities of the Mediterranean world, next only to Rome, Alexandria, and Antioch. Paul could rightly claim to be the "citizen of no mean a city" (Acts 21:39).

The city owed its importance not only to its geographical position but also to its recent history. Cilicia had long been a battle ground between the surrounding Hellenistic kingdoms before it

1

came under Roman control in 103 BCE when Marcus Antonius Orator conducted a victorious campaign against the pirates who had taken shelter in Cilician coves and bays. Should we say that Cilicia fell under the Roman yoke or that it entered the protective fold of *Pax Romana*? Provinces had to pay heavy taxes to Rome, but Rome assured security to business and trade. We may likely presume that Tarsian weavers and traders preferred to be under Roman authority rather than being at the mercy of pirates' exactions. A few years afterward, in 85 BCE, they would have greeted with a sigh of relief the victory of Sulla over Mithridates, king of Pontus, who had attempted to add Cilicia to his kingdom.

In 64 BCE, Pompey conferred to Cilicia the status of Roman province. The leading classes of Roman provinces could claim Roman citizenship. According to the Acts of the Apostles, Paul's family was sufficiently affluent and socially positioned to claim the title (Acts 16:37; 22:27–29). It means also that the family had opted for integration in Greco-Roman society. It was this attitude inherited from the family background that finds an echo in the Apostle's advice to pay taxes and "pay to all what is owed to them: taxes to whom taxes are owed, revenue to whom revenue is owed" (Rom. 13:6–7). Paul did not intend to elaborate a treatise of political theology. He just gave the commonsense advice that guided family dealings.

The unification of the Mediterranean world and of western Asia under Roman control contributed to shape the mind of the young Tarsian. Tarsus was also known as a booming intellectual center. Strabo, the author of a world *Geography* toward the beginnings of the Common Era, wrote about the Tarsus people:

> The inhabitants of this city apply to the study of philosophy and to the whole encyclical compass of learning with so much ardor, that they surpass Athens, Alexandria, and every other place which can be named where there are schools and lectures of philosophers. It differs however so far from other places that the studious are all natives, and strangers are not inclined to resort thither. Even the natives themselves do not remain at home, but travel abroad to

complete their studies, and having completed them reside in foreign countries. Few of them return. . . . They have schools of all kinds, for instruction in the liberal arts.

Strabo follows with a list of Tarsian celebrities:

The Stoic philosophers Antipater, Archedemus, and Nestor were natives of Tarsus: and besides these, the two Athenodori, one of whom . . . was the preceptor of Cæsar, who conferred on him great honors. . . . These men were Stoics, but Nestor, of our time, the tutor of Marcellus, son of Octavia, the sister of Cæsar, was of the Academic sect. . . . Among the other philosophers . . . were Plutiades and Diogenes, who went about from city to city, instituting schools of philosophy as the opportunity occurred. Diogenes, as if inspired by Apollo, composed and rehearsed poems, chiefly of the tragic kind, upon any subject that was proposed. The grammarians of Tarsus, whose writings we have, were Artemidorus and Diodorus. But the best writer of tragedy, among those enumerated in "The Pleiad," was Dionysides. Rome is best able to inform us what number of learned men this city has produced, for it is filled with persons from Tarsus and Alexandria. Such then is Tarsus.[1]

Living in Tarsus could not but open the mind of its young citizen.

Pax Romana

Tarsus was flourishing at the time when Roman history had reached a glorious climax. Saul of Tarsus was born under the reign of the great Emperor Augustus, who ruled from 27 BCE to 14 CE. He was martyred under the reign of Nero in 67. His life and ministry correspond to the Julio-Claudian dynasty. This period, and especially the reign of Augustus, is the golden age of Roman history. The authority of Augustus, combined with his political acuteness, had put an end to the convulsions of the

---

1. Strabo, *Geography* 14.13–15.

republic and restored peace all over the empire. The boundaries of this empire spread out from the Atlantic Ocean to Mesopotamia, and its influence extended even beyond. As proudly proclaimed in the *Res Gestae Divi Augusti*, engraved on bronze tablets at the entrance of the emperor's mausoleum,

> I restored peace to all the provinces of Gaul and Spain and to Germany, to all that region washed by the Ocean from Gades to the mouth of the Elbe. . . . My fleet sailed along the Ocean from the mouth of the Rhine as far towards the east as the borders of the Cimbri. . . . On my order two armies were led . . . into Ethiopia and into Arabia which is called "the Happy." . . . Ethiopia was penetrated as far as the town of Nabata, which is near Meroe.[2] In Arabia, the army advanced into the territory of the Sabaei to the town of Mariba. In the case of Greater Armenia, I preferred to hand that kingdom over to Tigranes. . . . I recovered all the provinces extending beyond the Adriatic Sea, and Cyrenae. . . . I settled colonies of soldiers in Africa. . . . The Parthians, I compelled to restore to me the spoils and standards of three Roman armies. . . . Embassies were often sent to me from the kings of India. . . . Our friendship was sought, through ambassadors, by the Bastarnae and Scythians, and the king of the Sarmatians who live on either side of the river Tanais, and by the kings of the Albani and of Hiberi and of the Medes. . . .[3] From us the people of the Parthians and of the Medes received the kings for whom they asked.[4]

Young Saul was privileged in being born and brought up in this widened world which, without cancelling local particular-

---

2. Meroe, on the fourth cataract of the Nile, a former capital of the Nubian Dynasty; Nabata or Napata on the Upper Nile, some 300 kilometers north of Meroe; Mariba, presently Maribu in Yemen.

3. Bastarnae lived along the Danube, Scythians along the Don (River Tanais), Albani around the Caspian Sea, and Hiberi in present Georgia.

4. Text quoted in A. H. M. Jones, *A History of Ancient Rome through the Fifth Century*, 2. *The Empire* (New York: Harper & Row, 1970), 14–23.

isms, was not torn by narrow minded chauvinisms or aggressive forms of racism. When Paul speaks of unity in Christ, nationalist hostilities do not even come to his mind. He knows only of a single ethnic difference, that of Jews and Gentiles (Gal. 3:28). It is as though all the other ethnic oppositions had already been done away with by the *Pax Romana*.

The Diaspora

But the ethnic border between Jews and Gentiles, between Chosen People and *go'im* did subsist. The Jewish population scattered among the nations was quite substantial. The Dispersion had begun with the Babylonian Exile. It was followed by successive migrations caused by various social and political troubles. A more or less voluntary migration also engaged merchants, craftsmen, and mercenaries in foreign armies. It extended mostly eastward where, beyond Mesopotamia, it reached Media and Persia as illustrated in the books of Esther and Tobit.[5] In those countries it constituted a substantial minority.

It is generally reckoned that Jews could have numbered one million in the Parthian Empire. In Egypt, they would have also counted one million out of a population of seven million. In Alexandria, they formed the bulk of the population of two districts out of five, which leads to an estimate of two hundred thousand to four hundred thousand, depending on whether the total population of the town is reckoned to have reached seven hundred thousand or a million people. Another three to four million Jews lived in Asia Minor, Greece, Cyrenaica, and in a few Italian towns.[6]

---

5. The St. Thomas tradition presumes the existence of a Jewish community in India. Cochin Jews claim to have arrived in India together with King Solomon's merchants.
6. M. Stern, "Diaspora," in S. Safrai and M. Stern (eds.), *The Jewish People in the First Century* (Compendia Rerum Iudaicarum ad Novum Testamentum I/1; Assen: Van Gorcum, 1974), 117–215; E. Schürer and G. Vermès, *The History of the Jewish People in the Age of Jesus Christ*, 3/1 (Edinburgh: T. & T. Clark, 1986), 291–363; C. Saulnier and C. Perrot, *His-*

A letter of Agrippa I to Caligula, reported by Philo, makes a proud statement of this situation:

(Jerusalem) is the mother city, not of one country, Judaea, but of most of the others in virtue of the colonies sent out at divers times to the neighboring lands Egypt, Phoenicia, the part of Syria called Hollow and the rest as well and the lands lying far apart, Pamphylia, Cilicia, most of Asia up to Bithynia and the corners of Pontus, similarly also into Europe, Thessaly, Boeotia, Macedonia, Aetolia, Attica, Argus, Corinth and into most of the best parts of Peloponnese. And not only are the mainlands full of Jewish colonies but also the most highly esteemed islands of Euboea, Cyprus, Crete. I say nothing of the countries beyond the Euphrates, for except for a small part they all, Babylonia and of the other those where the land is highly fertile, have Jewish inhabitants.[7]

Carried by his enthusiasm, Philo goes to the extent of claiming that the children of Sarah formed "the most numerous nation on earth."[8] His claim may be overstated. But it did refer to a significant and influential Jewish presence in the Greco-Roman world

toire d'Israël, III. De la conquête d'Alexandre à la destruction du Temple (Paris: Cerf, 1985), 287; P. Trebilco, *Jewish Communities in Asia Minor* (SNTSMS 69; Cambridge: Cambridge University Press, 1991); L. H. Fledmann and M. Reinhold (eds.), *Jewish Life and Thought among Greeks and Romans: Primary Readings* (Minneapolis: Fortress, 1996); I. Levinskaia, *The Book of Acts in Its Diaspora Setting* (Grand Rapids: Eerdmans, 1996); J. M. G. Barclay, *Jews in the Mediterranean Diaspora: From Alexander to Trajan (323BCE–117CE)* (Edinburgh: T. & T. Clark, 1996).
    7. Philo, *Legat.* 281–82; cf. *Flacc.* 45–46.
    8. *To polyanthrōpopaton tōn ethnōn* (*Congr.* 3). "The multitude which constitutes this people is such that, unlike other nations, it could not be contained within the confines of a single territory. It had to spread all over the world for it spread throughout all the continents and all the islands to such an extent that it seems almost to outnumber local population" (*Legat.* 214).

and beyond. It did not function as a secluded ghetto and did not adopt the warlike stand of the Maccabees in Palestine. Living in symbiosis with the surrounding peoples, Diaspora Judaism was necessarily conditioned by this daily sharing with the life and culture of these lands. It followed the advice once given by Jeremiah to the Babylonian exiles: "Build houses and live in them; plant gardens and eat their produce. . . . Seek the welfare of the city where I have sent you into exile, and pray to the Lord on its behalf, for in its welfare you will find your welfare" (Jer. 29:5–7). However, integration did not mean assimilation. Though merged into the surrounding world, the Jewish Diaspora remained solidly attached to its spiritual roots. Hostile reactions did take place. Philo himself recalls a pogrom that happened in Alexandria in 37 A.D.[9]

Alexandria was the most active center of the Diaspora. Its community spoke and wrote in Greek. It produced an extensive Greek literary output. To explain the Jewish Law to the Hellenistic world, Philo wrote seventy-seven treatises of unequal length in Greek. Other Jewish writers like Aristoboulos, Artapan, Aristeas, and Ezekiel the Tragedian tried to connect the Law of Moses with the Egyptian and Greek wisdoms. The Wisdom of Solomon was received in the Alexandrian canon.

The most outstanding work of the Hellenistic Diaspora was the Greek translation of the Bible called the Septuagint. Moving from Hebrew to Greek was a risky venture. A typical instance is the translation of YHWH as *kyrios*, Lord. The cryptic tetragrammaton carried an aura of mystery. This aura was lost in the Greek translation of "Lord, master," which could apply to any superior being, pagan god, emperor, or simply house lord. So, it was also for the translation of *Torah* as *nomos*. The *Torah* was grace and revelation: it expressed the way in which God guided his Chosen People with infinite love. The *nomos* was the rational law, social expression of the *logos*. Substituting *nomos* for *Torah*

---

9. Philo, *Flacc.* 29.

amounted to a secularization of social life. We understand the lament of an old rabbi. "The day when the Bible was translated into Greek was as disastrous as the day of the Golden Calf."[10] Yet this semantic loss was the cost to pay if the biblical message could enter the vast world of nations, and not appear like the strange dialect of an obscure West Asian tribe.

In Corinth, Paul met a representative of this Diaspora in the person of Apollos, an Alexandrian Jew converted by Aquila and Priscilla (1 Cor. 1:12; 3:5–6; cf. Acts 18:24–28). However, the Jewish community of Tarsus would have been more closely connected with their neighbors in Antioch than with Alexandria.

The Antiochian Diaspora was as important as that of Alexandria. As reported by Josephus,

> The Jewish race, densely interspersed among the native populations of every portion of the world, is particularly numerous in Syria, where intermingling is due to the proximity of the two countries. But it was at Antioch that they specially congregated, partly owing to the greatness of that city, but mainly because the successors of King Antiochus enabled them to live there in security. For, although Antiochus surnamed Epiphanes sacked Jerusalem and plundered the Temple, his successors on the throne restored to the Jews such votive offerings as were made of brass, to be laid up in their synagogue, and, moreover, granted them citizen rights on an equality with the Greeks. Continuing to receive similar treatment from later monarchs, the Jewish colony grew in numbers, and their richly designed and costly offerings formed a splendid ornament to the temple. Moreover, they were constantly attracting to their religious ceremonies multitudes of Greeks, and these they had in some measure incorporated with themselves.[11]

10. Quoted by E. Nida, *Towards a Science of Translating* (Leiden: Brill, 1964), 2.

11. Josephus, *Jewish War* 7.43–44 (trans. H. S. J. Thackeray; Loeb Classical Library; Cambridge, MA: William Heinemann, 1961).

However, important as it was, the Antiochian Diaspora does not seem to have equaled Alexandria in intellectual creativity. Was it because it was more conservative in outlook? Were the family of Saul and their co-religionists of Tarsus particularly "zealous for the ancestral traditions" (Gal. 1:14)? At the risk of being anachronistic, can we say that Alexandria stood for some form of liberal Judaism whereas Antioch was more orthodox? It may be rather that, belonging to the same Semitic linguistic area as Palestine, Syrian Antioch did not feel so acutely the need for acculturation. It had no need of a Septuagint Greek version; Aramaic targums were sufficient. As for Paul, his attitude toward the Greco-Roman world is not "Alexandrian." When compared with the Judaism of Alexandria, he appears to be an "abnormal" representative of the Diaspora. But, actually, he was more an Antiochian than an Alexandrian Jew.

Formation

The first setting of young Saul's education was the complex framework of a Jewish Diaspora of the Antiochian type, living in the midst of Hellenistic culture and well integrated in the socio-economic life of the Roman Empire.

At Home

According to Acts 18:3, Saul's family ran a small business of *skēnopoioi*. Literally the word means "tent makers." But the term extended to the weaving of any kind of canvas-covering goods in ships and chariots, to festive hangings and even to the vast *velum* that sheltered big meetings from sun and rain. Tarsus was a center of the textile industry. Goats of Anatolia and flax from Cicilia provided its workshops with needed raw material.[12] Young Saul grew up in this familial and social setting. From the family workshop he received a professional training that he will use to sup-

---

12. J. Murphy-O'Connor, *Paul: A Critical Life* (Oxford: Clarendon, 1996), 32–70.

port his apostolic campaign.[13] The family business taught him
also to run a budget and turn money into an apostolic tool.[14]

Paideia

From the Hellenistic milieu of Tarsus, he received a good Greek
education. How long did he stay in Tarsus and at what age was he
sent to Jerusalem? The question is debated. One opinion is that
he would have been sent to Palestine at an early age to shelter him
from Hellenistic contamination.[15] But the general opinion is that,
as a teenager, he was in Tarsus and had the same schooling as any
youth belonging to a well-to-do family. What is sure is that the
Greek he writes is good, educated Greek. It has a rich vocabu-
lary. It uses the resources of Greek rhetoric. The syntax is correct
unless he gets excited! His letters follow the structure of classical
epistolography, even though he does not remain corseted by the
structure.[16] The influence of prevailing Stoicism can occasionally
be perceived (Gal. 5:19–23; 1 Cor. 7:32–34).[17]

A re we to imagine young Saul attending the local high school?[18]
Or was he sent for private coaching to a grammatist who, for
a few coins, would teach the children of the neighborhood? Or

---

13. O'Connor, *Paul: A Critical Life*, 170–71.

14. O'Connor, *Paul: A Critical Life*, 89.

15. Such is the opinion of W. C. Van Unnik, "Tarsus or Jerusalem, the
City of Paul's Youth," in *Sparsa Collecta*. *Part One* (Leiden: Brill, 1973),
259–320, on the basis of Acts 22:3. "Brought up in this city" (of Jerusalem)
would imply that Saul's family returned to Jerusalem at an early stage and
that he "spent all the years of his youth in Jerusalem" (p. 296). Whatever
may be the semantic value of Van Unnik's interpretation of the participle
anatethrammenos ("brought up"), can we take at its face value Luke's rendering of what could have been Paul's speech at that time? In general, Van
Unnik's opinion has not been retained.

16. Van Unnik, *Sparsa Collecta*, 172–74.

17. On the influence of the Greco-Roman context on Paul, see L.
Legrand, *The Bible on Culture* (New York: Orbis Books, 2000), 127–51,
and the papers of the 62nd Colloquium biblicum lovaniense, *Paul's Graeco-
Roman Context* (ed. C. Breytenbach; BETL 277; Leuven: Peeters, 2015).

18. O' Connor, *Paul: A Critical Life*, 49–51.

again, was Saul's family sufficiently affluent to own an educated slave to serve as a pedagogue to the family children?[19] At any rate, it appears that young Saul's childhood and early youth in Tarsus imbibed him with the wider horizons of the Greco-Roman world. Living in Tarsus, following the Hellenistic schooling cursus, sharing in the open atmosphere of Mediterranean Diaspora, reading the Greek Bible of this Diaspora, the young Tarsian, even though unawares, was being readied to become a minister to the nations.

Jerusalem

Open as it was to the world at large, the Jewish Diaspora remained all the same faithful to its religious roots. Saul's family did not only abide by its Jewish faith, it remembered also with pride its belonging to the tribe of Benjamin. In each generation, it gave one of its sons, probably the eldest one, the name of the most famous representative of the tribe, King Saul, who had been anointed by Prophet Samuel as the first king of Israel. The family sympathized with the movement of the Pharisees and its strict obedience to the demands of the Law. It will remain a matter of pride for Paul the Apostle who will boast of being "a Pharisee, a son of Pharisees" (Acts 23:6; cf. Phil. 3:5–6).

This zeal for the Law took him to Jerusalem in quest of a rabbinical formation "at the feet of Gamaliel" (Acts 22:3). There could not have been a better master. Gamaliel was a highly reputed rabbi. He belonged to the liberal tendency as opposed to the rigorous interpretations of Shammai. The Acts report an example of his tolerant attitude toward the budding Christian movement (Acts 5:34–39). However, young Saul does not seem to have inherited this open-minded attitude. He describes himself as an extremist, "advancing in Judaism beyond many of my own age among my people, so extremely zealous was I for the traditions of my fathers" (Gal. 1:14). The stay in the Holy City hard-

---

19. M. F. Baslez, *Saint Paul*, 40.

ened this "zeal." His character was too passionate and his youth too fiery to adopt an indulgent position. The Acts describe him as "breathing threats and murder against the disciples of the Lord" (Acts 9:1). He committed himself fully to the fight against Jesus's followers and sided with Stephen's executioners. He might have been too young to be on the front row and was only entrusted with looking after the garments of those who were throwing the stones. But he was not too young to be put in charge of the posse sent to put an end to the Christian movement in Damascus. He acknowledges it with humility: "I persecuted the church of God" (1 Cor. 15:9).

Even though he did not share in the moderate stand of his master, he received at least a solid rabbinical training. While his style and thought were imbibed with Greek culture, his heart and mind remained fundamentally Jewish. As a good Jew and a trained rabbi, he based his arguments on Scripture and applied them to the text with the help of midrashic techniques. When we read his comments on Exodus in 1 Corinthians 10:1–10, we feel like we are sitting in the synagogue listening to the Sabbath sermon. As for the discussion on the two wives of Abraham in Galatians 4:21–31, it recalls the rabbinical debates in which learned doctors of the Law exchanged ever more sophisticated speculations on the text.

Mostly and more deeply, Saul inherited from his family and from his Jerusalem studies a passionate attachment to his people, Israel. It will remain engrained in the soul of the Apostle. Even when facing the sorrowful failure of the gospel among the Jews, he will keep his sense of Israelite identity:

> I am speaking the truth in Christ—I am not lying; my conscience bears me witness in the Holy Spirit—that I have great sorrow and unceasing anguish in my heart. For I could wish that I myself were accursed and cut off from Christ for the sake of my brothers, my kinsmen according to the flesh. They are Israelites, and to them belong the adoption, the glory, the covenants, the giving of the law, the worship, and the promises. To them belong the patriarchs, and from their

race, according to the flesh, is the Christ who is God over all, blessed forever. Amen. (Rom. 9:1–5)

This is no renegade language. Paul's faith in the Risen Christ remains through and through a Jewish faith.

Birth and childhood in a practicing Jewish family, early youth in the context of a Diaspora coexisting with the Hellenistic world, rabbinical formation in Jerusalem under famed rabbis, all these factors combined together in the mind and heart of young Saul. His style will weave together Hellenistic rhetorical skill and rabbinical subtlety. But it was mostly his mind that benefited from this rich multiculturalism. Two main directions will result: a visceral attachment to the people of Israel and a readiness to meet the Hellenistic world. Saul may not have been aware of it, but the Spirit was preparing him as a chosen instrument to bring to the Greco-Roman world faith in Jesus Christ, the Messiah promised to Israel and to the world.

PART ONE

The Envoy, the Messenger, and the Message

Paul, a Servant of Christ Jesus, Called to Be an Apostle, Set Apart for the Gospel of God (Romans 1:1)

Such are the words by which Paul states his identity to the Christians of Rome. He is somewhat unknown to them; he had not evangelized them. Since he wants to meet them and get their support to spread the gospel to Spain, he must introduce himself. Concise as it is, this self-description covers the three main aspects of his apostolic identity. 1. He has been sent and set apart. 2. The envoy is qualified as "apostle" and "servant." 3. He is entrusted with a message, the Good News. Such are the three main directions that the following chapters will explore to identify the Apostle and the mission entrusted to him by the Risen One, met on the road to Damascus.

2

"Set Apart and Sent"

The liturgical calendar celebrates the "Conversion of St. Paul" on January 25. Many painters have depicted the event, often adding a horse to the biblical text in order to enhance Paul's fall.[1] The phrase has become proverbial: of a convert it is said that he had a road-to-Damascus moment. However, unlike other translations (NLT, ESV, etc.), the NAB and the NJB have another caption: "the Vocation of Paul." Conversion or vocation? Change of religion or call to mission? What was the main significance of the encounter of the young Pharisee with the Jesus whom he persecuted? We must leave it to Paul to answer. He refers to the event several times. In conclusion, a comparison with Luke's viewpoint in Acts will help to specify better the Pauline focus.

Paul's Witness

In his letters, Paul refers several times to his encounter with the Risen Lord.

---

1. The horse seems to appear in Christian iconography in the twelfth century, under the influence of chivalry. See F. Boespflug, "La conversion de Paul dans l'art médiéval," in *Paul de Tarse* (ed. J. Schlosser; LD 165; Paris: Cerf, 1996), 155–59. Previously, Byzantine art depicted Paul on foot, falling down in the midst of his companions (pp. 147–53).

Reveal His Son in Me, in Order that I Might Preach Him among the Gentiles (Galatians 1:16)

In the beginning of the letter to the Galatians, to prove the divine origin and authority of his gospel, Paul gives a vivid report of his meeting with the Risen Christ.

> For you have heard of my former life in Judaism, how I persecuted the church of God violently and tried to destroy it. And I was advancing in Judaism beyond many of my own age among my people, so extremely zealous was I for the traditions of my fathers. But when he who had set me apart before I was born, and who called me by his grace, was pleased to reveal his Son in me, in order that I might preach him among the Gentiles, . . . I went away into Arabia and returned again to Damascus. (Gal. 1:13–17)

Paul presents a contrasting picture opposing the hostility of the persecutor to the divine election. It was not Paul who was in search of God but God in search of Paul, like the Good Shepherd chasing the lost sheep.

The Apostle realizes that "God had set him apart before he was born." He refers to two Old Testament texts:

> Before I formed you in the womb, I knew you, and before you were born I consecrated you; I appointed you a prophet to the nations. (Jer. 1:5)

> The Lord called me from the womb, from the body of my mother he named my name. . . . And now the Lord says, he who formed me from the womb to be his servant, to bring Jacob back to him; and that Israel might be gathered to him . . . he says: "It is too light a thing that you should be my servant to raise up the tribes of Jacob and to bring back the preserved of Israel; I will make you as a light for the nations, that my salvation may reach to the end of the earth." (Isa. 49:1, 5–6)

Paul views himself as carrying out the mission announced by the prophets. The Risen One entrusts him with a mission and makes him the prophet of the last times who will bring light to the nations. This light is the revelation of the Son of God: (God) "was pleased to reveal his Son in me, in order that I might proclaim him among the Gentiles." Each word is to be considered:

- *Reveal:* in the literal sense of unveiling. What was confused and obscure in the faith of Saul the Pharisee is now enlightened when this faith is transfigured, and its significance illuminated. In 2 Corinthians 3:13–18, Paul will describe more elaborately this luminous experience of unveiling, of shedding a veil.
- *His son*: Rabbi Saul considered the Nazarene as a false prophet whose deceiving ways had been unmasked, as a reprobate accursed by being "hanged on a tree" (Gal. 3:13). He is now manifested as the "Son of God," the ultimate representative of God's wisdom and power (1 Cor. 1:23).
- *In me*: and not simply "to me" as several versions have it (RSV, ESV, NAB, NLT). It is an internal experience reaching his deepest self. The Damascus encounter is no simple "vision." If the apostolic ministry will "reflect the glory of the Lord," it is because the Apostle himself is "transfigured into the same image" (2 Cor. 3:17) in the depth of his heart.
- *That I might proclaim him*: the "revelation" must be shared; light must shine. The internal revelation is not self-centered. God does not want only to change the heart of the persecutor. He wants to make him an apostle. As for the prophets, the Word is received to be message. The grace of illumination entails marching orders.
- *Among the Gentiles*: according to the prophets, on the last days, the nations would be gathered with the People of the Covenant (Isa. 2:3 = Mic. 4:1–3; Isa 42:6; 49:6; 60:2–6, 19–20; Zech. 8:22). The same expectation was also expressed in the Psalms (87; 96:7–9; 99:2–3). For Paul, the Resurrection of the Messiah means that the times have come to extend to all the peoples the promises and the covenant according to Hosea's prophecy:

"Those who were not my people I will call 'my people,' and her who was not beloved I will call 'my beloved.' And in the very place where it was said to them, 'You are not my people,' they will be called 'sons of the living God'" (Rom. 9:25–26 = Hos. 2:25). The Risen One ushers in the end of times when the nations are invited to join the lineage of Abraham, not by genetic belonging but by sharing the faith of Abraham (Gal. 3:6–9; Rom. 4:1–25). Paul's specific mission will make him the agent of this universalism.

Am I Not an Apostle? Have I Not Seen Jesus Our Lord? (1 Corinthians 9:1)

In a single sentence, this short text summarizes the significance of the encounter with the Risen Jesus. "I have seen Jesus *our Lord*." Paul does not speak only of a visual experience: he has seen Jesus *as the Lord*. As in Galatians 1:16, in Jesus risen again, he had the revelation of the Son of God. On the face of Jesus, he has perceived the illumination of the glory of God (2 Cor. 4:6). Seeing "Jesus our Lord" means discovering "the power of his Resurrection" (Phil. 3:10), the power and wisdom of God manifested in the folly and the weakness of a crucified Messiah.

All of Us, with Our Unveiled Faces like Mirrors Reflecting the Glory of the Lord, Are Being Transformed into the Image that We Reflect in Brighter and Brighter Glory

(We are) not like Moses who put a veil over his face so that the Israelites should not watch the end of what was transitory. But their minds were closed; indeed, until this very day, the same veil remains over the reading of the Old Testament: it is not lifted, for only in Christ is it done away with. As it is, to this day, whenever Moses is read, their hearts are covered with a veil, and this veil will not be taken away till they turn to the Lord. . . . And all of us, with our unveiled faces like mirrors *reflecting* the glory of the Lord, are being transformed into the image that we reflect in brighter and brighter glory; this is the working of the Lord who is the Spirit. (2 Cor. 3:13–18)[2]

The apostle defends the authenticity of his ministry by explaining what the "conversion to the Lord" is in the light of his personal experience. He did not take to another religion but, according to the meaning of the Greek verb *epistrepsē*, he "turned toward the Lord." He did not turn away from his faith in the God of Sinai. On the contrary, his encounter with Christ revealed the full meaning of that faith. It was an unveiling. His explanation follows the rabbinical method of *midrash*, explaining the text by actualizing it. According to the Book of Exodus, it was given to Moses to abide with God on Mount Sinai. He came down from the mountain haloed with the divine glory that surrounded him. This irradiation was so dazzling "that the Israelites could not gaze at Moses's face because of its glory" (2 Cor. 3:7; cf. Exod. 34:29–30) and Moses had to put a veil on his face to spare those who surrounded him (Exod. 34:33–34). Paul resumes this image and turns the veil into a symbol of darkened perception. The veiled glory shining round the mediator of the Law is nothing when compared with the glory revealed in Christ. This is the fiery glory that Paul has been given to contemplate. He has been transfigured by it, and his ministry is its reflection. This ministry of the gospel, "ministry of the new covenant, not of the letter but of the Spirit, of the life giving Spirit" (2 Cor. 3:6) is recorded "not with ink but with the Spirit of the living God, not on tablets of stone but on tablets of human hearts" (2 Cor. 3:3). It is a "glorious ministry" which reflects like a mirror the glory of the Lord (2 Cor. 3:18).

---

2. We follow the translation of the NJB rather than the ESV. In v. 18, the translation "reflecting" is preferred (cf. NIV, NLT) rather than "contemplating" (NAB, NRSV). The Greek verb is ambiguous, but, in the context, Paul speaks of the personal experience that made him an apostle rather than of Christian life in general.

The Glory of God in the Face of Jesus Christ

> For God, who said, "Let light shine out of darkness," has shone in our hearts to give the light of the knowledge of the glory of God in the face of Jesus Christ. (2 Cor. 4:6)

Then, resuming the midrashic explanation of the unveiling of the glory of God, he applies it to the "face of Christ." It is on the face of Christ that, out of darkness, shines the light "for the nations" and reaches "the end of the earth" (cf. Isa. 49:6). The contemplation of this face gives the true "knowledge of the glory of God." The face of Christ is the face of the Risen One, but it is also, and it remains, the face of the Crucified One. Having the "knowledge of the glory of God" consists also in "knowing nothing except Jesus Christ and him crucified" (1 Cor. 2:2). More than the thunders and the lightnings of Sinai, the face of the one who was crucified and has risen again is the ultimate theophany. God reveals his deepest being on the face of his Son. This theophany is interior: "it has shone in our hearts." But contemplation results in mission: "to give the light of the knowledge" of what is really "the glory of God."

For His Sake I Have Suffered the Loss of All Things . . . , in Order that I May Gain Christ

> But whatever gain I had, I counted as loss for the sake of Christ. Indeed, I count everything as loss because of the surpassing worth of knowing Christ Jesus my Lord. For his sake I have suffered the loss of all things and count them as rubbish, in order that I may gain Christ and be found in him, not having a righteousness of my own that comes from the law, but that which comes through faith in Christ, the righteousness from God that depends on faith that I may know him and the power of his Resurrection, and may share his sufferings, becoming like him in his death. (Phil. 3:7–10)

The encounter with the Risen One was for Paul a stirring experience of illumination. But it was also a radical upheaval of his deepest self. "The power of the Resurrection" undermines the basis on which the life of Rabbi Saul was built. It is a conversion but in the internal sense of the term as expressed by the Greek word *metanoia*. The *noia*, that is the mental set up (*nous*), the sense of values, whatever one has in mind and heart, undergoes a radical *meta*-static experience, of turning upside down, of total upheaval. Elsewhere Paul will express in vigorous terms what that upheaval means in terms of the value systems of Greece (wisdom) and of Israel (power of signs):

> Jews demand signs and Greeks seek wisdom, but we preach Christ crucified, a stumbling block to Jews and folly to Gentiles, but to those who are called, both Jews and Greeks, Christ the power of God and the wisdom of God. For the foolishness of God is wiser than men, and the weakness of God is stronger than men. (1 Cor. 1:22–25)

The capacity of the poor human heart is too limited to receive divine transcendence and especially the transcendence of divine love as expressed in a crucified Messiah. The human heart is broken open and shattered by the impact of this love. So was Paul's heart. We can speak of a conversion of Paul but not in the sense of a change of religion. It was in his deepest self that Paul was transformed and transfigured by the encounter with Christ.

Conclusion

For Paul, the encounter with the Risen One was *revelation* in the literal sense of the term as an unveiling. It lifted a veil on the hidden depths of his faith in the God of Israel and on the project of God toward his people. It was an *illumination*: the Resurrection of the one who had been crucified manifested a God of love, of a mad love, as shown by the madness of the Cross. On the face of him who had been crucified and had risen again, Paul discovered the true splendor of the glory of God. Revelation and illumination lead to *mission*. They were given to Paul so that he might be the prophet who "announces the Son" and "gives the light of the knowledge of the glory of God" manifested "in the face of Jesus Christ."

It was an *upheaval* of all that young Saul considered as his Israelite identity. He does not see it now as based on the Law but on the Spirit as prophets had announced already. What made one a son of Abraham was not the "flesh" but "faith in him who raised from the dead Jesus our Lord" (Rom. 4:24). The covenant is the new covenant that God writes in the heart of his people (Jer. 31:33). God will communicate his own Spirit, give a new heart and a new spirit, and take away the heart of stone to replace it by a heart of flesh (cf. Ezek. 36:26; Ps. 51:12–13).

This new covenant was now open to the *universalism* of the last days since the Resurrection of the Son of God means that the plenitude of times has come when all the nations would be called to join God's people. "Minister of the New Covenant" in the Spirit, Paul is entrusted with the responsibility and the authority of "Apostle to the Nations" (Rom. 11:13), invested with the mission to gather them in faith to the Good News. His is not the authority of a human master but the authority of the Lord himself. It is an *apostolic* authority, the authority of the gospel (Gal. 1:8–9).

Referring to Jeremiah and to the Servant of Yahweh, Paul views himself as belonging to the lineage of the prophets of Israel. But within this lineage, his vocation is specific. It is not conferred by prophetical succession as in the case of Elijah and Elisha or of the "sons of the prophets" (2 Kgs. 2:1–8). It comes directly from the Risen Lord. The Good News that the Apostle receives and communicates is the ultimate fulfillment of the plan of divine love in the world. The Apostle is the eschatological prophet who brings to bear on present days, through the proclamation of the Good News, the impact of the ultimate event of the Resurrection of the Messiah.

Paul may not have perceived at once and clearly all the dimensions of his encounter with the Risen Lord. When he reported his vocation to the Galatians, the Philippians, and the Corinthians, he did it with the benefit of hindsight and of a reflection fed by fourteen years and more (Gal. 2:1) of painful failures and unexpected successes. But this reflection only deepened the primordial experience of illumination and ultimate revelation received when he met the Risen Lord.

The Account of Acts

Paul's own report of his encounter with the Risen Lord remains the primary witness. However Christian imagination and imagery know the event mostly through the report that Luke gives in Acts (9:1–19; 22:3–21; 26:9–18). Is Luke a faithful interpreter or does he betray his model? The difference of literary form is to be taken into account. Whereas Paul reports the event in an introspective mood, Luke writes as a historian, "the historian of God."[3] Paul's witness goes to the depth of the soul. Luke's report is colorful. It has inspired many a painter. However, despite formal differences, the following points of agreement can be retained.

- The importance of the event is scored by Luke in a triple report in the same way as Paul recalls several times the event that changed his life.
- Under different forms, Paul and Luke adopt a similar structure based on the contrast between the fanatic persecutor and the disciple who has been won over. The verb "persecute" (*diōkō* in Greek) occurs equally in Acts (9:4, 5; 22:4, 7, 8; 26:14, 15) and in Paul (1 Cor. 15:9; Gal. 1:13, 23; Phil. 3:6) to characterize the attitude of Saul, the zealous Pharisee.
- Just as Paul speaks of "illumination," Acts describes "the light from heaven [that] flashed around him" (Acts 9:3; 22:6; 26:13).
- In Acts as in Paul's letters, the mission of the Apostle is described in terms of the vocation of Jeremiah (Acts 9:15; 26:17

---

3. As per the title of the original French book of D. Marguerat, translated in English as *The First Christian Historian* (SNTSMS 121; Cambridge: Cambridge University Press, 2002).

= Jer. 1:5, 10) and of the Servant called to be a witness to bring light to the nations (Acts 26:16–18 = Isa. 49:6).

- In Acts as in Paul, the main accent is laid on the mission, and the mission field entrusted to Paul is the world of the nations (Acts 9:15; 22:21; 26:17 = Gal. 1:16).

These are essential points of agreement. We may even wonder whether Luke did not refer to Paul's letters when writing his story. Yet differences between Luke and Paul are not negligible.

Whereas Paul insists on a mission received directly from Jesus Christ (Gal. 1:1), Acts lays a stress on the human mediation of Ananias (9:10–19; 22:12–21). This corresponds to the "importance of mediations" in Lukan theology in the framework of his theology of the church.[4] For Paul, the "revelation" is internal ("*in me*," Gal. 1:16). It is a transforming revelation (2 Cor. 3:18) that affects his inmost being. Luke gives these ideas a picturesque form, but the spiritual depth is veiled as much as expressed by those images, and the message is reduced to the mission (Acts 9:16; 22:15; 26:17). Luke's account loses in interiority what it gains in colorful impact.

The main difference consists in the fact that, for Luke, the encounter with the Risen Christ does not make Paul an "apostle." He is a "chosen instrument" (9:15), a "witness" (22:15; 26:26), a "servant" (26:26). In Acts, the qualification of "apostle" is reserved to the Twelve who have accompanied Jesus "from the baptism of John till the day when he was taken up" (1:22). Their role is to be the link between the time of Jesus and the apostolic period of the direct witnesses. In the structure of Acts, Paul's function is rather to be the prototype of the post-apostolic period, which is the time in which Luke's readers live. Luke is the theologian of the period that extends presently until the parousia. It is the time of the mission of the church. For Luke, Paul belongs to that time and stands out as a model for us who, like him, belong to that time.

---

4. Cf. F. Bovon, "L'importance des médiations dans le projet théologique de Luc," *NTS* 21 (1974): 23–39.

In short, Luke proposes a hermeneutic interpretation of Paul. He translates the unique revelation and mission received by Paul in terms of the ongoing times. For Paul, the encounter with the Risen Christ was an "apocalypse," the ultimate unveiling of God's plan. Luke turns it into an image of Paul as a model for missionaries. He can be blamed for making banal the significance of Paul. He can as well be praised for providing the reader with an example to follow. But we have always to return to Paul himself to reach, at the heart of the mission, the meaning of the unique encounter with the One who had been crucified and was risen from the dead.

Luke stirs the imagination. Paul goes to the heart, the heart of what he experienced, and the heart of the mission entrusted to him. The literary framework and the life setting differ. However, both Luke and Paul view the Damascus encounter as a vocation story and a call to mission. It implied a conversion, but it was not a "conversion to Christianity." It is a conversion to a new life in "the power of the Resurrection." For both, mission is not "propaganda" but communion.

3

The Messenger: Apostle

The encounter with the Risen One does not make Paul a convert but a messenger, an apostle entrusted with a mission. "Apostle" is the term used by Paul to introduce himself to those to whom he writes (Rom. 1:1; 1 Cor. 1:1; 2 Cor. 1:1; Gal. 1:1). Against his opponents he defends his right to be called an "apostle." What did he mean when using this qualification? How did his readers understand it?

The Word "Apostle"

The original meaning of the word "apostle" is problematic. The Greek word *apostolos* is evidently connected with the verb *apostellein*, to send. Etymologically the *apostolos* refers to somebody who is sent. But in common usage, the word was applied rather to an expeditionary force or task force and to its commanding officer. In commercial terms, the word applied to the bill, the "invoice," or to the receipt. This common use has little to do with "the apostle of the gospel." Rabbinical writings mention the institution of the *shelihim* (from the verb *shalah* to send). It referred to the disciples whom the rabbi sent and commissioned through the laying on of hands. This would apply to the disciples sent by Jesus. But this rabbinic institution does not seem to have appeared prior to the second century CE and so it would have been later than New Testament times. In Hellenistic

Judaism, the use of *apostolos* is rare.[1] So the semantic origin of the word "apostle" remains obscure, and its frequent use in the sense of messenger of the gospel seems to be typical of Christian language.

The Christian use of the word is complex. Originally, the Twelve chosen by Jesus are not called "apostles."[2] Their role is to be "Twelve," like the twelve patriarchs, the ancestors of the twelve tribes of Israel (Gen. 49:1–27). They represent the new patriarchate based on faith and not on ethnic descent. It was Luke who amalgamated the two terms and made the Twelve as the twelve apostles (Acts 6:13; 9:10; 17:5; 22:14; 24:10). In the election of Mathias, Peter lists the conditions required to be an "apostle," a privileged witness of the Risen Lord. He must "have accompanied us during all the time that the Lord Jesus went in and out among us, beginning from the baptism of John until the day when he was taken up from us" (Acts 1:21–22). Paul does not meet these requirements, and Luke will be careful to avoid giving this title to Paul.[3] But Luke's writings are later than Paul. The Pauline claims to be an "apostle" appears first in the Pauline writings themselves and that in 1 Thessalonians 2:6, in the first Pauline letter, and the very first writing of the New Testament.

---

1. "In the 1st century *apostolos* is rare in literary language; unknown to Philo, it is used only once by Josephus and once only also in the LXX ... (1 Kgs xiv, 6)" (C. Spicq, *Notes de lexicographie néo-testamentaire supplément* [OBO 22/3; Fribourg: Éditions Universitaires; Göttingen: Vandenhoeck & Ruprecht, 1982], 56). Cf. L. Cerfaux, "Pour l'histoire du titre *apostolos* dans le Nouveau Testament," in *Recueil Lucien Cerfaux: Études d'exégèse et d'histoire religieuse* (BETL 18; Gembloux: Duculot), 1962, 2:185–86.

2. In Mark 6:30, Matthew 10:2, and Luke 9:10, the Twelve are called "apostles." But this qualification does not go back to Jesus himself, as shown by J. Dupont, "Le nom d'apôtres a-t-il été donné aux Douze par Jésus?" in *Études sur les évangiles synoptiques* (BETL 70B; Gembloux: Duculot, 1985), 2:1007–9.

3. The lone exception is Acts 14:4 where the title is given in the plural to Barnabas and Paul in the general sense of "missionaries."

The use of the term in this context shows that it was already part of the Christian language. It could have the general sense of "delegates of the churches" sent to remit the funds collected in favor of the poor of Jerusalem (2 Cor. 8:23). Andronicus and Junia are "prominent among the apostles (Rom. 16:7)."[4] The list of witnesses of the Resurrection in 1 Corinthians 15 distinguishes the Twelve associated with Cephas (v. 5) and "all the apostles" connected with James, the brother of the Lord (v. 7). However, in other texts, the word "apostle" carries overtones of special responsibility and authority. In the list of spiritual gifts and ministries of 1 Corinthians 12, the "apostles" come first (v. 28) before prophets and doctors though without reference to the Twelve, absent in Corinth. In the autobiographical report of Galatians 2, Paul specifies that, after encountering Christ, he did not meet "those who were apostles before" him. Later on, he "saw none of the other apostles except James the Lord's brother" (Gal. 1:17–19). At the Jerusalem Assembly the role of those "pillars" is important: without their approval, he would have "run in vain" (Gal. 2:2). The role of Peter is qualified with the technical term of *apostolē*, which suggests a specific position.

Apostolic Legitimacy

Paul applies the same technical term *apostolē* to his ministry (Rom. 1:5; 1 Cor. 9:2; Gal. 2:8). On what grounds could he do it? How could he compare, if not identify, his *apostolē* with that of Peter? Whence the assurance with which he introduced himself to the Romans as one "called to be apostle" (Rom. 1:1)?

We have to return to the short but revealing text of 1 Corinthians 9:1 in which he defends his apostolic identity against the opponents. "Am I not an apostle? Have I not seen Jesus our Lord? Are not you my workmanship in the Lord?" The context is noteworthy. The legitimacy of his apostleship is questioned by opponents who accuse him of being a fraud. He replies with a double argument. First, he has seen Jesus our Lord. Second, the

---

4. NAB translation. The ESV has only "well known to the apostles."

existence of the community is the living proof that his ministry is genuine.

Have I Not Seen Jesus Our Lord?

As seen above, in the illumination of his encounter, Paul has recognized Jesus as *the Lord*. But the reverse is equally true: it is *Jesus* who has been recognized as the Lord. By using the verb "to see" and specifying that the Lord he recognized was indeed *Jesus*, Paul stresses the corporal character of his encounter with the Lord. It was not a dream, an ethereal vision, a purely internal illumination. He met a bodily Risen One. Later on, Paul will reflect on the nature of this risen body (1 Cor. 15:35–48). Anyway, it was indeed Jesus and not a ghost. As regards his apostolate, this direct bodily encounter has put Paul on an equal footing with the "other apostles" (9:5). These "other apostles" and the brothers of the Lord were privileged in having been the companions of Jesus, his intimate associates. Paul did not enjoy this physical association. The grace of God has led him straightaway to the intimacy with the Risen One. He is but an "untimely born" (1 Cor. 15:8). Yet he did see "Jesus," and, though belatedly, he has been associated with the corporeal Jesus. This is why he shares in the responsibility and the authority of the "other apostles."

Are Not You My Workmanship in the Lord?

The very existence of the community of faith in Corinth is another proof of the authenticity of Pauline apostleship: "Are not you my workmanship in the Lord? If to others I am not an apostle, at least I am to you, for you are the seal of my apostleship in the Lord. This is my defense to those who would examine me" (1 Cor. 9:1–3). The "signs of apostleship" can be seen in the fruits it has born (1 Cor. 3:6), the emergence of a community of believers among the nations. The unexpected response to the Good News among the pagans confirms the authenticity of Paul's apostolate. It is the "seal" affixed by God on the credential letters of his messenger. The faith of the Corinthians proves that the foundations laid by the Apostle are truly the work of Christ, the true temple where the Spirit of God abides (1 Cor. 3:10–17). Faith in Jesus Christ among the pagans is the letter of assignment of the divine legate, signed by the Holy Spirit:

> Do we need, as some do, letters of recommendation to you, or from you? You yourselves are our letter of recommendation, written on our hearts, to be known and read by all. And you show that you are a letter from Christ delivered by us, written not with ink but with the Spirit of the living God, not on tablets of stone but on tablets of human hearts. (2 Cor. 3:1–3)

"They Gave the Right Hand of Fellowship to Barnabas and Me" (Galatians 2:9)

To make sure that he "did not run in vain" (Gal. 2:2), Paul gets his apostolate to the pagans endorsed by the mother church of Jerusalem and its "pillars." James, Cephas, and John recognize the validity of Pauline apostleship as equivalent to that of Peter among the Jews. The agreement is solemnly sanctioned by "giving the right hand of fellowship" (Gal. 2:9). This does not mean that Paul is commissioned by them through delegation. From the beginning of the letter, he has insisted that he is "an apostle, not from men nor through man, but through Jesus Christ and God the Father, who raised him from the dead" (Gal. 1:1). He distances himself "from those who seemed to be influential" (Gal. 2:6). However, he does not reject them. He remains in communion with the "pillars." Yet, his *apostolē* does not come from them but from Christ himself.

Apostolic Identity

Of what does this *apostolē* consist?

Ambassador

The role of Paul is well expressed by the word "ambassador": he is the "ambassador of Christ":

> All this is from God, who through Christ reconciled us to
> himself and gave us the ministry of reconciliation; that is, in
> Christ God was reconciling the world to himself, not count-
> ing their trespasses against them, and entrusting to us the
> message of reconciliation. Therefore, we are ambassadors for
> Christ, God making his appeal through us. We implore you
> in the name of Christ, be reconciled to God. (2 Cor. 5:18–20)

The word "ambassador" brings out the two opposite aspects of
the function. The ambassador holds a subordinate position. He
is not like the founder of a philosophical school who parades an
impressive originality of thought. The ambassador does not speak
in his own name. The apostle speaks "in the name of Christ."
Paul insists: "It is God who makes his appeal through us." The
ambassador is only the mouthpiece of a superior authority. On
the other hand, the ambassador is invested with the dignity and
the authority of the mandating power. "The apostle gives himself
a title of nobility, for a legate is a noteworthy personage, at the
top of the military hierarchy, and *presbeuō* and *presbeutēs* are
technical terms for imperial legates in Greek Orient."[5]

The message brought by Paul as an "ambassador for Christ" is
a message of love and reconciliation between God and the human
sinner. The initiative comes from God: "God in Christ was recon-
ciling the world to himself not counting their trespasses against
them." God himself fulfilled the conditions for this reconciliation
by sending "the one who knew no sin" to be "made sin for our
sake so that in him we might become the righteousness of God"
(2 Cor. 5:21). The sinner has only to surrender to the embrace
of the Father as the prodigal child of the parable. By entrusting
the Apostle with the message of reconciliation, God has given
him the ministry of reconciliation. "Mission, proclamation of the
Gospel are at the heart of reconciliation. As a direct witness, the
apostle authenticates it in his person and his message."[6]

---

5. C. Spicq, art. *presbeuō*, *TLNT*, 558.
6. M. Carrez, *La deuxième épître de Saint Paul aux Corinthiens* (CNT
8; Geneva: Labor et Fides, 1986), 153.

The Identity Card of the Apostle

The letter to the Romans gives Paul an opportunity to introduce himself as an "apostle." By the time he writes the letter he has accomplished a long ministry. Therefore, it is the fruit of all his reflections on the meaning of his ministry that he summarizes in a few condensed verses. This was called for by the situation. The Roman community was not the outcome of his work. They might have heard of him, but he was an outsider. Since he wants to visit them and get their support for a drive to Spain, he has to introduce himself to justify his intervention. This is the reason for an exceptionally long *intitulatio*, or identification of the writer. It counts 71 words.[7] It can be called the apostolic identity card that he produces to the community he intends to visit.

> Paul, a servant of Christ Jesus, called to be an apostle, set apart for the gospel of God, which he promised beforehand through his prophets in the holy Scriptures, concerning his Son, who was descended from David according to the flesh and was declared to be the Son of God in power according to the Spirit of holiness by his Resurrection from the dead, Jesus Christ our Lord, through whom we have received grace and apostleship to bring about the obedience of faith for the sake of his name among all the nations, including you who are called to belong to Jesus Christ. (Rom. 1:1–6)

The structure of this introduction is significant. The self-introduction of the Apostle in verses 1 and 5 frame a summary of the "gospel of God," the Good News concerning Jesus Christ, son of David according to the flesh and Son of God according to the Spirit. The gospel of God constitutes the heart of the apostolic identity: the messenger is defined by the message. The Apostle has no other raison d'être than the gospel. He is identified by the

---

7. Cf. 1 Thessalonians (5 words), 1 Corinthians (12 words), 2 Corinthians (11 words), and Galatians (26 words).

gospel. It is not enough to say that he must devote all his energy to the proclamation of the Good News. He is inhabited by the "power of the gospel." It is the gospel that makes an apostle and is the soul of his mission. Verses 1 and 5 present the qualifications that justify the title of "apostle."

- The first qualification is to be *called*. The initiative does not come from the apostle: he is "called." As the vocation narrative of Galatians 1 had concluded: "the gospel that was preached by me is not man's gospel. For I did not receive it from any man, nor was I taught it, but I received it through a revelation of Jesus Christ" (Gal. 1:11–12).
- *Set apart*: Galatians 1:15 is more explicit: "set me apart before I was born" (Gal. 1:15), like Jeremiah (1:15) and the Servant of the Lord (Isa. 49:1).[8] The apostle is a successor to the prophets. His message, "promised beforehand through his prophets in the holy Scriptures," is no individual ideology. It belongs to the divine plan on the world.
- *To proclaim the gospel of God*: as seen above, God has revealed to Paul that the one who had been crucified and risen again is the Son of God, the ultimate expression of the love of God for the world, and of the victory of this love over the powers of death, dawn of a new life. Such is the Good News which is to be shared with the world. Chapter 5 will return to the contents of the Good News.
- *Through whom we have received grace:* the autobiographical account of Galatians 1:15–16 also laid a stress on divine grace: "he who called me by his grace, was pleased to reveal his Son in me, in order that I might preach him among the Gentiles" (Gal. 1:15–16). It is in the name of the "grace given [him] by God" that he calls to unity the Romans prone to division and that he dares to do it "very boldly" (Rom. 15:15). It is this grace of his apostolate to the Gentiles that James, Cephas, and John will acknowledge (Gal. 2:9). Full meaning should be given to what

---

8. Carrez, *La deuxième épître de Saint Paul aux Corinthiens*, 30, 37.

Paul says about the origin of his vocation: "by the grace of God I am what I am, and his grace toward me was not in vain. On the contrary, I worked harder than any of them, though it was not I, but the grace of God that is with me" (1 Cor. 15:10). This statement says it all: the apostolic boldness and the awareness that the source of strength is not his. He does not mean only that the grace of God helped him to be a good apostle. His thought goes deeper. It is the grace of God that makes him an apostle. It is at the origin and remains at the heart of his mission. It gives him boldness (*parrhēsia*) (1 Thess. 2:2; cf. 2 Cor. 3:12; 7:4; Phil. 1:20; Acts 28:31) and "capacity to hold fast (*hypomonē*) in afflictions, hardships, calamities, beatings, imprisonments, riots, labors, sleepless nights, hunger" (2 Cor. 6:4–5). Everything is grace. For Paul, mission is grace before being a charge; it is a gift received before being engagement in action.

- *To bring about the obedience of faith for the sake of his name*: the apostolic mission does not consist in enlisting adepts. It calls to *faith*; that is to the deep internal transformation of the whole being implied in the filial *obedience* and commitment to the divine project of a new creation. The ultimate aim is that everything turns to the *glory of his name*, that "every tongue may confess that Jesus Christ is Lord, to the glory of God the Father" (Phil. 2:11).
- *Among all the nations*: it is the specific mission of Paul. We shall return to it in chapter 6. Entrusted with this mission he can address the Roman Christians who, to a large extent, had come from paganism.

A main feature characterizes this identity card of the apostle. It presents an identity made of alterity. Alterity of God who, by his grace, is the origin of the mission and who is also the end of the mission meant "to the glory of his name." Alterity of the nations called to respond to the Good News through the "obedience of faith." Paul does not introduce himself in terms of personal qualifications and still less on the basis of his successful ministry in

Asia Minor, Macedonia, Corinth, and Ephesus. What makes the apostle is self-surrender in response to God's grace and the dedication that made him to "become all things to all people (1 Cor. 9:22)." Mission is oblation (Phil. 2:17).

Apostolic Authority

Church Founder and Leader

When Paul calls himself an apostle, he does not mean only that he is a missionary. He applies the tile to himself in the full sense of *church founder and leader*. He calls himself "the least of the apostles," unworthy of the title. He speaks with humility, but the underlying implication is that a real dignity is attached to the title of apostle. Elsewhere he assumes the title with "pride" (*kauchēsis*) (Rom. 15:17; 2 Cor. 1:12; 7:4; 11:10, 17; Phil. 2:16; 3:3). Others claimed the title, though they were unworthy of it; and Paul will oppose those "superapostles" (2 Cor. 11:5), "false apostles, deceitful workmen, disguising themselves as apostles of Christ" (2 Cor. 11:13). As for him he has too lofty a sense of what his apostolic mission signifies to give way to vainglory. The themes he associates with his apostolic identity show how deep this sense is.

Exercise of Authority

The grace of God that constitutes him as an apostle confers on him authority (*exousia*) (1 Cor. 9:4–6, 12, 18; 2 Cor. 10:8; 13:10), an authority that is not his own but that of an "ambassador of Christ" (2 Cor. 5:20).[9] 1 Corinthians illustrates all along the exercise of this authority. The young church met with a number of problems and was subject to divisions and misconceptions. With the authority of the founder, Paul enlightens,

---

9. Cf. J.-N. Alettti, "L'autorité apostolique de Paul. Théorie et pratique," in *L'apôtre Paul: Personnalité, style et conception du ministère* (ed. A. Vanhoye; BETL 73; Leuven: University Press, 1986), 229–46; J.-C. Ingelaere, "Paul et l'exercice de l'autorité apostolique," in *Paul de Tarse* (ed. J. Schlosser; LD 165; Paris: Cerf, 1996), 119–46.

corrects, and decides. Thus in a matter of incest in chapter 5, he convokes a meeting where, "spiritually present," (v. 4), he will preside over and "as if present," he will have "already pronounced judgment on the one who did such a thing" (1 Cor. 5:3). In 2 Corinthians, he defends his authority passionately to the point of speaking of "jealousy" (2 Cor. 11:2). The last part of the letter (chaps. 10–13) is an impassioned plea against those who question his authority. However, he insists that it is not his personal position but the truth of the gospel that is at stake (Gal. 1:6–10; 1 Cor. 4:1–5).

In a Spirit of Agapē

His is no despotic authority. It is exercised with "the meekness and gentleness of Christ" (2 Cor. 10:1) in a spirit of *agapē*. Before being the eulogist of love in 1 Corinthians 13, Paul puts *agapē* at the heart of his apostolate. Examples are many. The "salutations" that conclude the letters to the Romans and to the Corinthians, and even the short note to Philemon, evoke a vast network of friendship that underpins the Pauline mission. Chapter 9 will treat of these coworkers of Paul. For Paul, they are not underlings who interest him only insofar as their work serves his purpose. For each one of them he has a particular word that reveals a personal link. The case of Persis is moving (Rom. 16:12). Her name shows that she is a slave. She is even deprived of the dignity of having a name. She is only Persis, the Persian girl, with reference to the country she comes from. Yet she is entitled to a special mention: she is "the beloved (*agapētos*) Persis," and she has the merit of having "worked hard in the Lord." The nameless poor slave must have been deeply moved to find her name mentioned along such lordly figures as Aristobulus and Narcissus, or Herodion, connected with the famed clan of the Herods.

The communities that he founded were his "beloved children," whose father he has become in Christ Jesus through the gospel (1 Cor. 4:15; cf. 1 Thess. 2:11). Already in his first letter, he considers himself not only as a father but even as a mother:

Though we could have made demands as apostles of Christ, we were gentle among you, like a nursing mother taking care of her own children. So, being affectionately desirous of you, we were ready to share with you not only the gospel of God but also our own selves, because you had become very dear to us. (1 Thess. 2:6–8)

"Gentle," "affectionate," "dear to us": these are terms of motherly endearment. At the outset of his ministry among the nations, Paul sets right his position as an apostle. He does not take a patronizing attitude. His ministry will be a love story. This love will be a source of worries. When intruders come to interfere with his apostolate, he feels "jealous," like a father who has betrothed his child and sees her attracted by others:

For I feel a divine jealousy for you, since I betrothed you to one husband, to present you as a pure virgin to Christ. But I am afraid that as the serpent deceived Eve by his cunning, your thoughts will be led astray from a sincere and pure devotion to Christ. (2 Cor. 11:2–3)

The Galatian community is still more worrisome. It has begun following false teachers and forsaking the gospel of freedom in Christ (Gal. 1:6–7). The letter he sends them combines the severity of apostolic authority with fatherly affection. He chastises them in stern terms: "O foolish Galatians! Who has bewitched you? It was before your eyes that Jesus Christ was publicly portrayed as crucified. . . . Are you so foolish? Having begun by the Spirit, are you now being perfected by the flesh?" (Gal. 3:1–4). He then shifts to another tone. He reminds them of the kindness they showed when he fell sick (Gal. 4:13–15) and moves to the bold image of the woman in birth pangs: "my little children, for whom I am again in the anguish of childbirth until Christ is formed in you!" (Gal. 4:19). It is the language of the heart, but, as rightly noted by C. Tassin, we must go beyond a purely sentimental interpretation: "It refers to the mystery of life giving, summarized in the words 'death is at work in us, but life in you'

(2 Cor. 4:12). This antithesis of life and death, which theologians call "the paschal mystery," is the heart of Paul's conception of apostleship."[10]

Conclusion

The word "apostle" belongs to the early beginnings of Christian language. It can be used in the general sense of delegate or worker at the service of the gospel. However, we see the emergence of its specific application to influential personalities who draw their authority from their early acquaintance with Jesus and their encounter with the Risen Lord. The Jerusalem community gathers around them; through the Diaspora, it will soon extend beyond Judaea. Though a late comer, and unrelated to the original clan, Paul sees his position as related to theirs. He too has known Jesus, if not as a Galilean, at least as the Crucified One. He too has met the Risen One who has entrusted him with the Good News of a new world and of a new life. He too, by virtue of this mandate, is invested with an authority that is not his own but the authority of the gospel. The specificity of his apostleship will be to extend it to the nations. Its canonical shape is not yet well determined. There will be conflicts, like the Antiochian quarrel (Gal. 2:11–14) and settlements like the Jerusalem agreement on respective fields (Gal. 2:9). Nevertheless, this mandate is unique like that of the other witnesses to the Resurrection.

Luke will limit the apostolic function to the Twelve: they will be the only "apostles" (Acts 1:21–22). By so doing, he altered radically Paul's mission. Paul is no longer an "apostle." He now represents the post-apostolic period when the mission does not come from the Lord but is received through the church. This appears clearly in the episode of the investiture of Paul and Barnabas described in Acts 13:1–3. The context is important: it relates to the inauguration of the Pauline mission. The Spirit takes the ini-

---

10. C. Tassin, *L'apôtre Paul: Un autoportrait* (Paris: Desclée de Brouwer, 2009), 12.

tiative, but the Spirit speaks and acts through the community: "Set apart for me Barnabas and Saul for the work to which I have called them" (Acts 13:2). The verbs "set apart" and "call" are the same as in Romans 1:2. On both sides, the call comes from God or his Spirit. But in Romans 1:2, God acts directly whereas, in Acts 13, the Spirit entrusts both choice and call to the church. It will be so for the generations to come. Luke has transformed Paul the Apostle into the typical missionary. It is Acts that presents Paul as a model for missionaries of future generations. But it is Paul himself who leads us to the luminous mystery that is the heart of the apostolic mission.

4

The Messenger: Servant and Slave

The Apostle announces the "gospel, power of God," energized by the "power of the Resurrection," "power of the Spirit." Is not this language of "power" too triumphalist? It "boasts" with "pride" of its divine origin and claims "authority." Is it not a show of arrogant self-conceit? Reflecting divine light, haloed with the glory of God and sent to carry this light to the nations, Paul could have made it a matter of self-glory, as the Gnostics who vaunted the superiority of their *gnosis* over the ignorance of common folk.

This is poles apart from the attitude of Paul. On the contrary, he experiences the contrast between the divine glory and his poor human opacity. Immediately after having evoked "the light of the knowledge of the glory of God" which "has shone in our hearts," he proceeds to add: "But we have this treasure in jars of clay, to show that the surpassing power belongs to God and not to us" (2 Cor. 4:6–7). God acts through human agents; the power comes from him. Declining his identity in Romans 1:1, Paul adds the added qualification of Servant to the title of Apostle. It is the other face of his apostolic identity. These two aspects of apostolic identity are intricately connected. The Servant is servant of Jesus Christ and thus partakes of the dignity of the Lord who sends him. On the other hand, the Apostle fulfills his mission of messenger of the Good News as the representative of Jesus the Servant in a spirit of servanthood.

The Servant

Dissensions between Christians in Corinth provide Paul with the opportunity to clearly state his subordinate position. The community is divided because its members commit themselves to one or the other of their evangelizers, either to Apollos, or to Kephas, or to Paul. But who are they? A variety of words and comparisons will emphasize their subordinate position. They are ministers, assistants (*diakonos*) (1 Cor. 3:5), underlings (*hyperētēs*) (1 Cor. 4:1),[1] and caretakers (*oikodomos*) (1 Cor. 4:1–2). They are like farm hands who plant and water whereas only God provides growth (1 Cor. 3:5–7). At best, they are like architects who make plans whereas the whole building rest on the one foundation stone, Christ (1 Cor. 3:10–11).

The word minister (*diakonos*) (2 Cor. 3:6; 6:4; 11:24) is particularly apt to express the position of the apostle. His role is to serve (*diakonein*) (2 Cor. 8:19–20). His function is *diakonia*, service of the Spirit (2 Cor. 3:7; 3:18–4:1), of reconciliation (2 Cor. 5:12), of justice (2 Cor. 3:9). The term carries overtones of both responsibility and subordination. There is no ground for pride. "For who sees anything different in you? What do you have that you did not receive? If then you received it, why do you boast as if you did not receive it?" (1 Cor. 4:7). This verse begins a section that Cerfaux entitles "the antinomy of apostolic life."[2] Corinthians found their pride in their new "knowledge" of the divine mysteries and in the charismatic gifts that they liked to display. Paul reacts ironically: "Already you have all you want! Already you have become rich! Without us you have become kings! And would that you did reign, so that we might share the rule with you!" (1 Cor. 4:8). He compares himself to one sentenced to death and paraded before his execution (4:9). Carried away by the thought, he goes to the

---

1. *Hyperētēs* comes from *hypo* (under) and *eretēs* (oarsman). Etymologically the word refers to the galley slave who pulls at the oars at the bottom of the trireme. Then the meaning extended to any subaltern position.

2. L. Cerfaux, "L'antinomie de la vie apostolique," in *Recueil Lucien Cerfaux: Études d'exégèse et d'histoire religieuse*, 2:455–67.

extent of declaring: "We have become, and are still, like the scum of the world, the refuse of all things" (1 Cor. 4:13). But amid his trials the servant continues to serve: "we labor, working with our own hands. When reviled, we bless; when persecuted, we endure; when slandered, we entreat" (1 Cor. 4:12–13). It is more than Stoic *ataraxia*, the capacity to control one's feelings. It is the expression of "life in Christ," of the grace of being moved by the Spirit of the Servant. The Pauline *diakonia* and his radical commitment to service recall the words of Jesus expressed in identical terms in Mark 10:45 (cf. Matt. 20:8): "the Son of Man came not to be served but to serve, and to give his life as a ransom for many." The "ministry" of the son of Man was "service" and gift of self until death. Paul may have known this saying of Jesus.[3] Anyway, he lived according to it.

The Slave

The word *doulos* (servant, slave) expresses unambiguously this radical surrender in service. It is the second element of the apostolic identity in Romans 1:1: "Paul, *doulos* of Jesus Christ, called to be apostle." It is Paul's favorite term to express his role. In the beginning of Philippians, it is even the only qualification. When his apostolic position is contested, it is on the basis of this term that he defends it: "If I were still trying to please man, I would not be a *doulos* of Christ" (Gal. 1:10). He has "enslaved" himself to the service of the gospel (Phil. 2:22). Faithful to the master, the Pauline tradition continues to see in this title the basic identity of the apostle (Titus 1:1; Acts 16:17).

But at the outset, a problem of translation arises. Should *doulos* be rendered as servant or as slave? The difference is important.

---

3. Before they were put in writing in the gospels, Jesus's words circulated in Christian communities, either in oral form or through small collections of *logia*. In this way, Paul might have come to know fragments of Jesus's teaching. Cf. F. Siegert, "Jésus et Paul: Une relation contestée," in *Jésus de Nazareth: Nouvelles approches d'une énigme* (ed. D. Marguerat, E. Morelli, and J.-M. Poffet; Geneva: Labor et Fides 1998), 448–51 with a table of contacts on p. 449 and a rich bibliography.

Spicq is unambiguous: "It is wrong to translate *doulos* as servant as it misses the exact meaning it had in 1st century language."[4] In Roman law, the meaning is clear: it knew only of two categories of persons: the free man and the slave. The condition of the slave is to be "an object of possession (*res mancipi*). Being a slave means being attached to the master by a bond of subjection."[5] Philosophy justified this position by considering it as a law of nature.[6] The word *doulos* recurs several times in texts dealing with slavery (1 Cor. 7:21–23; 12:13; Gal. 3:28; cf. Eph. 6:5; Titus 2:9). In the moral sense, it refers to enslavement to corruption (Rom. 8:21), to sin (Rom. 6:6, 17), to false gods (Gal. 4:8). According to Spicq, "slave of Jesus Christ" must be understood in the sense of surrender of one's autonomy, of integral abandon of one's will. In a similar way, when Paul tells Corinthians that he is their "slave in Jesus Christ," he does not mean only that he is their servant who will help them to the best of his abilities. He does mean that he is their "slave," that he has given himself over completely to them and belongs to them. He has no other interest at heart than theirs. As he wrote to them: "all things are yours, whether Paul or Apollos or Cephas . . . all are yours" (1 Cor. 3:21–22).

However, an important precision is to be added. The apostolic enslavement is no "natural" imposition. It is a voluntary option, a gift of self in love. Alienation of will is real but freely surrendered. The enslavement is radical, but it is oblation and consecration.

---

4. C. Spicq, art. *doulos, TLNT,* 167.

5. Spicq, *doulos,* 167.

6. "It is also nature which, in order to preserve the order of things, has created some beings to command and others to obey. It is nature which intended that those endowed with foresight should be in a commanding position as masters and that those endowed with physical abilities to implement these commands should obey as slaves so that, finally, the interest of the master and of the salve complement each other. Therefore, nature has determined the special condition of women and of slaves" (Aristotle, *Polit.* 1.4–5). In Galatians 3:28, Paul contradicts this "natural" view: "There is neither Jew nor Greek, there is neither slave nor free, there is no male and female, for you are all one in Christ Jesus." He applies this principle to the case of Onesimus, the young runaway slave, whom he kept with him (Phlm. 16).

When the Shulamite of the Song of Songs says, "My beloved is mine" (Song 2:16), she speaks of real dispossession as a slave owner would say of what he considers to be his livestock. But she adds immediately, "and I am his." It is a joyful fusion of liberties in love. This mutual oblation is worlds apart from the situation of the slave harnessed to the grinding stone. Taking into account this ambiguity attached to the terminology of enslavement, we cannot exclude totally the words "servant" and "service." But, when translating *doulos* as "servant," we must keep in mind that the "service" is unto life and death and that the "slave" has surrendered to the Lord with all his heart and all his soul.

The word *doulos* appears in its most tragic meaning of debasing enslavement in its application to the Passion of Christ in Philippians 2:5–8:

> Have this mind among yourselves, which is yours in Christ Jesus, who, though he was in the form of God, did not count equality with God a thing to be grasped, but made himself nothing, taking the form of a servant, being born in the likeness of men. And being found in human form, he humbled himself by becoming obedient to the point of death, even death on a cross.

Christ as *doulos* evokes the Servant of the Lord in Isaiah 53:12, who "poured out his soul to death . . . , bore the sin of many, and makes intercession for the transgressors." But, connected with the cross, a punishment reserved to slaves, a *servile supplicium*, the term takes a connotation of degrading slavish position. Dying crucified, Christ forfeited everything to render the ultimate service. The Greek verb (*kenoō*) suggests emptiness (*kenos*), the total loss of honor. Theology uses the word kenosis in the sense of complete dispossession. On the cross, God dispossesses himself of glory to manifest himself in the final theophany of sacrificial love.

Such is the example that Paul proposes to the Philippians, who were too eager to vaunt their ego:

> Be of the same mind, having the same love, being in full accord and of one mind. Do nothing from rivalry or conceit, but in humility count others more significant than yourselves. Let each of you look not only to his own interests, but also to the interests of others. Have this mind among yourselves, which is yours in Christ Jesus. (Phil. 2:2–5)

There is no other glory than the glory of serving and, for Christ, serving meant the Cross.

Apostolic Kenosis

This is what Paul lived. It was the heart of his apostolic kenosis: "Far be it from me to boast except in the cross of our Lord Jesus Christ, by which the world has been crucified to me, and I to the world. . . . I bear on my body the marks of Jesus" (Gal. 6:14, 17). Elsewhere to the Corinthians, to vindicate the authenticity of his apostolic ministry, he writes:

> Always carrying in the body the death of Jesus, so that the life of Jesus may also be manifested in our bodies. For we who live are always being given over to death for Jesus' sake, so that the life of Jesus also may be manifested in our mortal flesh. So, death is at work in us, but life in you. (2 Cor. 4:10–12)

"Death at work in us but life in you": thus did Paul identify with the mystery of the kenosis of the One who was the Slave unto death and death on a cross to be the firstborn of a new life.

However, two specifications are to be added to the image of Paul, "slave of Jesus Christ" and of the community. First it should be noted that this kenosis is not to be viewed as a goal to be reached through the arduous process of spirited ascetic efforts. His kenosis is essentially a gift of God. He says: "We share abundantly in Christ's sufferings" (2 Cor. 1:5), and the entire letter will spell out how he did it. But they are "Christ's sufferings," a gift that he receives to be united with Christ, gift of grace inherent to the experience of his weakness, his trials, and the failures of his ministry. His only title of glory and the proof of authenticity of his ministry is his weakness, which he assumes with humor when he describes the hero of the gospel comically escaping hidden in a basket (2 Cor. 11:32–33). The litany of his misfortunes can be read in 2 Corinthians 6:4–10; 11:23–33; and 12:7–9. They illustrate in his own case the great law of strength in weakness (1 Cor. 4:7–13). He mentions also in veiled terms a humiliating affliction that seems to have been a recurring annoyance. It may be the disease that landed him among the Galatians, and which could have raised "scorn and hatred" (Gal. 4:14). He leaves it to the imagination of readers and commentators to identify this trouble. He calls it "a thorn in the flesh, a messenger of Satan to harass me" (2 Cor. 12:7). He adds: "Three times I pleaded with the Lord about this, that it should leave me. But he said to me, 'My grace is sufficient for you, for my power is made perfect in weakness'" (v. 8). And he concludes in triumphant words: "Therefore I will boast all the more gladly of my weaknesses, so that the power of Christ may rest upon me. For the sake of Christ, then, I am content with weaknesses, insults, hardships, persecutions, and calamities. For when I am weak, then I am strong" (vv. 9–10). It is not in mystical ecstasy but in the upsets of daily life that Paul discovers the "power of Christ."

Another and most important observation is that Pauline kenosis is no nihilism. For Christ, kenosis leads to the exaltation and supreme lordship: "Therefore God has highly exalted him and bestowed on him the name that is above every name, so that at the name of Jesus every knee should bow, in heaven and on earth and under the earth, and every tongue confess that Jesus Christ is Lord, to the glory of God the Father" (Phil. 2:9–11). It is the triumph of what the Cross signifies: the ultimate power of love. Kenosis is not debilitating but enlivening humility. It does not annihilate human will but opens it to the transcendent power of divine will. The humility of the Servant does not lead to depression or indifference. It opens on the power of "him who is able to do far more abundantly than all that we ask or think, according to the power at work within us" (Eph. 3:20).

Paul has been accused of pessimism, of obsession with sin and misanthropy. Sure enough, during his ministry, he met with enough trouble not to take mission as a walk in the Garden of Eden. Mostly he had seen in the Crucified One the heart-rending image of sin and evil. But he had also seen the Crucified One as the One who had risen, as a source of divine power.

> We are afflicted in every way, but not crushed; perplexed, but not driven to despair; persecuted, but not forsaken; struck down, but not destroyed; always carrying in the body the death of Jesus, so that the life of Jesus may also be manifested in our bodies. For we who live are always being given over to death for Jesus' sake, so that the life of Jesus also may be manifested in our mortal flesh. (2 Cor. 4:8–11)

Therefore, we better speak of Pauline optimism. It is not the naïve optimism that says that everything turns out for the best in the best of all possible worlds. But Paul knows that "God works for good, for those who love him, who are called according to his purpose. For those whom he foreknew he also predestined to be conformed to the image of his Son, in order that he might be the first-born among many brothers" (Rom. 8:28–29). The image of his Son is the face of the One who was crucified and rose again, irradiating the glory of God. And "if God is for us, who can be against us? He who did not spare his own Son but gave him up for us all, how will he not also with him graciously give us all things?" (Rom. 8:31–32). In human frailty, God's power is at work: this is what Paul lived as a "slave of Jesus Christ, called to be an apostle."

Conclusion

Finally, more than the "signs and wonders," it is the intimate bond with the One who was crucified and rose again that accredits the Apostle. It is this "communion in his sufferings, becoming like him in his death" leading to "the power of his Resurrection" (Phil. 3:10) that recommends the Apostle and authenticates his ministry.

As servants of God we commend ourselves in every way: by great endurance, in afflictions, hardships, calamities, beatings, imprisonments, riots, labors, sleepless nights, hunger; by purity, knowledge, patience, kindness, the Holy Spirit, genuine love; by truthful speech, and the power of God; with the weapons of righteousness for the right hand and for the left; through honor and dishonor, through slander and praise. We are treated as impostors, and yet are true; as unknown, and yet well known; as dying, and behold, we live; as punished, and yet not killed; as sorrowful, yet always rejoicing; as poor, yet making many rich; as having nothing, yet possessing everything. (2 Cor. 6:4–10)

This bond underlies whatever the Apostle did and said. It was further strengthened by his ministry. The Acts of the Apostles gives a detailed report of Paul's journeys. The letters of the Apostle reveal another journey, an interior progress. The way to Damascus continued in the soul of the Apostle to the Nations. In the course of his mission progress, of the unfolding of his projects, of his successes and failures, the initial encounter with the Crucified-Risen One penetrated his heart more and more deeply and fashioned it at the image of the Master. John of the Cross has described the *Ascent of Mount Carmel* through the successive stages of the "dark nights of the soul." Paul followed a similar mystical ascent through the apostolic nights in which was realized a more and more effective "communion in his sufferings, becoming like him in his death," leading to "know the power of his Resurrection."[7] As Paul lived it, mission is a mystical way.

An essential characteristic of missionary spirituality is intimate communion with Christ. We cannot understand or carry out the mission unless we refer it to Christ as the one who was sent to evangelize. St. Paul describes Christ's attitude: "Have

---

7. Cf. D. Marguerat, "La mystique de l'apôtre Paul," in *Paul de Tarse* (ed. J. Schlosser; LD 165; Paris: Cerf, 1996), 307–26 with a bibliography p. 308.

this mind among yourselves, which is yours in Christ Jesus, who, though he was in the form of God, did not count equality with God a thing to be grasped, but emptied himself, taking the form of a servant, being born in the likeness of men. And being found in human form he humbled himself and became obedient unto death, even death on a cross" (Phil. 2:5–8).

The mystery of the Incarnation and Redemption is thus described as a total self-emptying which leads Christ to experience fully the human condition and to accept totally the Father's plan. This is an emptying of self that is permeated by love and expresses love. The mission follows this same path and leads to the foot of the cross.

The missionary is required to "renounce himself and everything that up to this point he considered as his own, and to make himself everything to everyone" (Vatican II, *Ad Gentes*, 24).[8]

---

8. John-Paul II, *Redemptoris Missio*, 88.

5

The Message:
The Good News

The Apostle-Servant is sent and mandated to transmit a message on behalf of God. It is the "Good News of God" (Rom. 1:1), not some good news but *the* Good News, final and absolute. It has divine authority since it is Good News *of God*. It is God who, through his messenger, addresses the message to his people. What is this message?

The Word

The word "gospel" appears frequently in the New Testament. The noun *euangelion* occurs 76 times; the verb *euangelizein*, 49 times. In Pauline writings, the noun is used 50 times and the verb, 21 times. It is a basic theme of Christian language and particularly of Pauline terminology. As Cerfaux said, "*euangelion* is definitely a Pauline term."[1] It summarizes the entire Pauline theology as it summarized the message of Jesus (Mark 1:14–15).

What does the word mean? The Greek word *euangelion* means "good (*eu*) news (*angelion*)" and so the verb *euangelizein* refers to the action that brings the "good news." In the Old Testament, the Hebrew noun *basorah* is rarely used (6 times). It applies only

---

1. L. Cerfaux, *Le Chrétien dans la théologie paulinienne* (LD 33; Paris: Cerf, 1962), 120.

to secular good news and has no religious connotation.[2] The use of the verb (*basar*) is more frequent. In general, it applies to all kinds of good news, concerning either public life, like announcing a victory or an enthronement, or private life, like a birth, a marriage, or any happy event. We shall come back to its specific use in the second part of Isaiah. The verb always reports concrete facts and "is always used in a context of joy."[3] It is not a "teaching" but the report of a fact.

We meet again here with a problem of translation. The English word "gospel" is usually applied to the four books of Matthew, Mark, Luke, and John. This meaning is later than the New Testament: it goes back to St. Justin (100–165 CE). Or it refers to the "teachings of Jesus Christ." But the word "teaching" betrays the basic meaning. The "gospel" is not "teaching" but "proclamation" of a joyful event. For Paul, this joyful event is the Resurrection of Jesus who had been crucified, the first fruits of the new creation. This is what Paul recalls to the Corinthians, quoting the faith confession which he has received: "Christ died for our sins in accordance with the Scriptures. He was buried, he was raised on the third day in accordance with the Scriptures" (1 Cor. 15:3–4). This is the essential message: "if Christ has not been raised, then our preaching is in vain and your faith is in vain" (1 Cor. 15:14).

"Set apart for the gospel," Paul does not receive the vocation of a theologian. He is called to bear witness to the event that has transformed his life, the encounter with the Risen One who had been crucified. The *evangelion* evokes a vital encounter and a deeply moving joy. The word "gospel" has lost these connotations.[4] However it does keep hallowed associations, and it cannot be totally excluded. The rendering "Good News" is preferable,

---

2. G. Friedrich, art. *euangelion*, *TDNT*, 2:721.

3. C. Spicq, art. *euangelion*, *TLNT*, 250.

4. The English word "gospel" comes from Old English *gōdspel* (*gōd* "good" + *spel* "news"). The Old English term was retained as "gospel" in Middle English and in Modern English.

but we cannot do without the traditional term of "gospel." Yet, when using the word "gospel," we should keep in mind the force of impact that it had for the Apostle.

A New Prophetical Language

If the language of the Good News is frequently used in the New Testament and can be considered as the focus of Jesus's and Paul's mission, it is not so in the Old Testament. Indeed, Good News represents a major turning point of biblical language. Prophetical language was made of judgment and of promise. The judgment bore on a past heavily loaded with its burden of sin. The promise concerned the future. The present hung between those two poles. With the Good News of Jesus Christ, the past is forgiven, and the joy of promised salvation is made present.

However, this change of perspective was already prepared in the Old Testament and particularly in Deutero-Isaiah, in what is called the Book of Consolation (Isa. 40–55). A few texts evoke already the Pauline message. Actually, they will be resumed in the New Testament.

In the context of the Babylonian captivity, God becomes the "Comforter." He announces the end of the exile and tells Sion to be the messenger of the "Good News" of the coming of the Good Shepherd.

> Comfort, comfort my people, says your God. Speak tenderly to Jerusalem, and cry to her that her warfare is ended, that her iniquity is pardoned, that she has received from the Lord's hand double for all her sins. . . . Get you up to a high mountain, O Zion, herald of good news; lift up your voice with strength, O Jerusalem, herald of good news; lift it up, fear not; say to the cities of Judah, "Behold your God!" Behold, the Lord God comes with might, and his arm rules for him; behold, his reward is with him, and his recompense before him. He will tend his flock like a shepherd; he will gather the lambs in his arms; he will carry them in his bosom, and gently lead those that are with young (Isa. 40:1–2, 9–11).

This is a remarkable text. It anticipates the language of the Good News. Usually the prophets viewed conversion as a preliminary condition to salvation: "'Return to me and I shall return to you!' says YHWH Sabaoth" in Malachi 3:7 (cf. Zech. 13:9). Even the message of the Baptist is in the same vein (Mark 1:4–5; Matt. 3:7–10). Indeed, Hosea had described the forgiveness of the unfaithful spouse (Hos. 2:16–25) and the fatherly affection of God toward his child, Israel. But this moving picture was framed by a set of diatribes against the crimes of Israel (Hos. 4:1–10:15; 12:1–14:1). With the Prophet of Consolation, the love of God precedes human response. Prophecy becomes Good News and shows an anticipated New Testament perspective. God's love is unconditional. Grace is a gratuitous gift. It is also a reversal of the God language. As the father of the prodigal son runs to meet the errant child, the Good Shepherd does not wait for the return of the lost sheep to take it on his bosom.

The same theme is resumed in Isaiah 52:7–10:

> How beautiful upon the mountains are the feet of him who brings good news, who publishes peace, who brings good news of happiness, who publishes salvation, who says to Zion, "Your God reigns." The voice of your watchmen— they lift up their voice; together they sing for joy; for eye to eye they see the return of the Lord to Zion. Break forth together into singing, you waste places of Jerusalem, for the Lord has comforted his people; he has redeemed Jerusalem. The Lord has bared his holy arm before the eyes of all the nations, and all the ends of the earth shall see the salvation of our God.

Paul resumes this text in Romans 10:15. The Hebrew and Greek texts mentioned a single messenger. By putting in the plural the *messengers* whose feet bring Good News, Paul enlarges the significance of the text. He has in mind the other apostles and the sway of "the word of Christ," which, through the apostolic preaching, "has gone out to all the earth, and . . . to the ends of the world" (Rom. 10:17–18).

In Isaiah 61, the context has changed. It is no longer Babylonia on the eve of the return to Jerusalem. The exiled have now returned to the Holy Land, but the country they find is impoverished. The Temple is a heap of ruins. The population is degenerate. The initial enthusiasm has cooled down. The People of God is a poor people. The Good News brought by the Messiah-Anointed, consecrated by the Spirit, is addressed to those poor and announces their liberation:

> The Spirit of the Lord God is upon me, because the Lord has anointed me to bring good news to the poor; he has sent me to bind up the broken-hearted, to proclaim liberty to the captives, and the opening of the prison to those who are bound; to proclaim the year of the Lord's favor, and the day of vengeance of our God; to comfort all who mourn. (Isa. 61:1–2)

This important text shows the emergence of a prophetical messianism after the exile. It will complement royal and priestly messianism. The Messiah is a prophet, and the kind of prophetism that the Spirit arouses is the announcement of the Good News. Jesus will have only to resume this text to present the main lines of his messianic mission in the synagogue of Nazareth (Luke 4:18).

The theme of the Good News found some echo in the messianic expectations of Israel. In the first century BCE, the Psalms of Solomon sing: "Blow you the trumpet in Sion to gather the saints! Proclaim the good news of the messenger in Jerusalem. God visits his people to show his grace" (Pss. Sol. 11:1–2). A puzzling Qumran text that takes Melchizedek as a messianic figure quotes explicitly Isaiah 52:7 and 61:1.[5] However, it cannot be

---

5. "These are the days of peace spoken by God through the prophet Isaiah who said: 'How beautiful on the mountain are the feet of the messenger announcing peace.' ... And this is the interpretation: the mountains are the prophets ... and the messenger is the Anointed of the Spirit" (11QMelch 15–18). See also the explicit reference to Isaiah 61:1 in 1QH XVIII.14.

said that the Good News constituted a major theme of Judaism during the Hellenistic period. The prophetic language remained comminatory and apocalyptic. Even for the Baptist, "conversion for the forgiveness of sins" is a prerequisite to the coming of the Messiah (Mark 1:4–5), and he condemns the "brood of vipers" that would not escape "the wrath to come" (Matt. 3:7).

It is all the more noteworthy to see the theme of the Good News resumed at the outset of the New Testament. There is no doubt that Jesus himself recognized his identity and his mission in the texts of Isaiah, which had largely fallen into oblivion. He made them the focal point of his message. Mark makes the Good News the header of whatever he will write about Jesus: "Jesus came into Galilee, proclaiming the Good News of God, and saying, 'The time is fulfilled, and the Kingdom of God is at hand; repent and believe in the Good News'" (Mark 1:14–15). In Luke, the text of Isaiah 61:1 is the starting point of the programmatic discourse of Nazareth (Luke 4:18–19). Also programmatic is the Sermon on the Mount in Matthew, which translates the Good News to the poor into Beatitudes (Matt. 5:3–10).

Good News of God. Good News of Jesus Christ

Paul also takes the Good News as the center of his message and of his mission. It is "the Good News of God" and the "Good News of Jesus Christ."

Good News of God

The Good News is "Good News of *God*" (1 Thess. 2:2, 8, 9; 2 Cor. 11:7; Rom. 1:1; 15:16, 19). In the subjective sense, it means that it comes from God: "Through us it is God who makes his appeal. We implore you on behalf of Christ, be reconciled to God. . . . Working together with him, then, we appeal to you not to receive the grace of God in vain" (2 Cor. 5:20–6:1). Therefore, the gospel proclaimed by the Apostle bears the seal of divine authority: "when you received the word of God, which you heard from us, you accepted it not as the word of men but as what it

really is, the word of God, which is at work in you believers"
(1 Thess. 2:13). Messenger of the Good News, the Apostle can
claim this authority: concluding 2 Corinthians in which he had
to vindicate his apostolic authority he evokes "the authority that
the Lord has given me for building up and not for tearing down"
(2 Cor. 13:10; cf. 2 Cor. 10:2, 8; 13:3). It was in the same terms
that prophetical authority had been given to Jeremiah (Jer. 1:10).

Good News *of God* is also to be understood in the objective
sense that it makes God to be known. The Good News of the crucified Messiah leads into the mystery of the "folly of God wiser
than men" (1 Cor. 1:25). It makes known

> a secret and hidden wisdom of God, which God decreed
> before the ages for our glory. None of the rulers of this age
> understood this, for if they had, they would not have cruci-
> fied the Lord of glory. But, as it is written, "What no eye has
> seen, nor ear heard, nor the heart of man imagined, what
> God has prepared for those who love him," these things
> God has revealed to us through the Spirit. For the Spirit
> searches everything, even the depths of God. (1 Cor. 2:7–10)

As Paul writes, in his conclusion to the letter to the Romans,
"The Good News I announce in preaching of Jesus Christ" refers
finally to "the revelation of the mystery that was kept secret for
long ages but has now been disclosed and through the prophetic
writings has been made known to all nations, according to the
command of the eternal God, to bring about the obedience of
faith" (Rom. 16:25–26).

Good News of Jesus Christ

The Good News is also the "gospel of the glory of Christ who
is the image of God" (2 Cor. 4:4). The gospel of God is therefore the "gospel of the Son" (Rom. 1:9), "the gospel of Christ"
(1 Cor. 9:12; 2 Cor. 2:2; 9:13; 10:14; Gal. 1:7; Phil. 1:27; 1 Thess.
3:2). "Gospel of Christ" means that it is Christ who has brought
the Good News: "For I would have you know, brothers, that the
gospel that was preached by me is not man's gospel. For I did

not receive it from any man, nor was I taught it, but I received it through a revelation of Jesus Christ" (Gal. 1:11–12). But, in the objective sense, it means also and mostly that the gospel has Jesus Christ as its object and main contents. As the prologue to Romans has it, it is "the gospel of God . . . concerning his Son, . . . Jesus Christ our Lord" (Rom. 1:1–4). The Good News is contained in the person of Jesus Christ: "I decided to know nothing among you except Jesus Christ and him crucified" (1 Cor. 2:2).

Paul has been criticized for this personification of Christian faith. Proclaiming the Good News of the Reign of God, Jesus opened the vast dimensions of God's plan for humanity and for the world. By sacralizing the person of Christ, Paul would have reduced these perspectives to the restricted dimensions of a confessional cult. By proclaiming Christ, he would have obliterated what Jesus proclaimed. Paul would have been responsible for the on-going disincarnated spiritualization of Christian faith. He would have distorted the message of the Galilean by reducing it to a sacred image. Beyond Paul, we would have to return to "Jesus before Christ" to recover the true Christian message.

These speculations misunderstand the significance that Paul attached to his encounter with the Risen One. The Jesus Christ who was the only thing that Paul wanted to know and proclaim is not disincarnated. It is Jesus, the Crucified One who assumed the tragedy of human existence defiled by sin (2 Cor. 5:21; cf. Gal. 3:13), subjected to the "bondage to corruption" and straining in the hope to "obtain the freedom of the glory of the children of God" (Rom. 8:21). For Paul, the encounter with the Risen Christ did not only change his mind as regards the one who had been crucified on Golgotha. In a larger perception, he saw in the Resurrection of Jesus the ultimate victory of the living God over the powers of death. Saul the Pharisee believed in the Resurrection (cf. Acts 23:6–8; 24:21) and saw it as the fulfillment of the prophecy of Ezekiel 37. The Spirit came on the dry bones and the people doomed to death came back to life (Ezek. 37:14). The Resurrection of Jesus did not mean only the return of the dead to life. It signified the end of the present age subject to evil (Gal.

1:4), enslaved to the oppressive powers of this world (Gal. 4:8–9; 1 Cor. 2:6). By the power of the Spirit, it marked the advent of a new people and the dawn of a new world (1 Cor. 15:20; cf. Rom. 8:23; 11:16). "As Christ was raised from the dead by the glory of the Father, we too walk in newness of life" (Rom. 6:4), in the "new life of the Spirit" (Rom. 7:6), "renewed day by day" (2 Cor. 4:16). In short, "if anyone is in Christ, he is a new creation. The old has passed away; behold, the new has come" (2 Cor. 5:17). The "new creation" evokes the apocalyptic expectation of "new heavens and a new earth" (Isa. 65:17; 66:22; cf. 2 Pet. 3:23; Rev. 21:1). The outlook is universal and cosmic.

The new life in the Spirit included all that the Reign of God signified. It transformed the individual, freeing him from the alienating forces of sin and death (Rom. 7:13–25). It brought about a new society that overcame the social fractures of race, class, caste, and gender (Gal. 3:28). The new world responded to the groanings of the "whole creation in the pangs of childbirth" (Rom. 8:22).

In a similar context of eschatological expectation, the Synoptic Gospels express the same joyful faith when they focus the teaching of Jesus on the "Reign of God." The Reign of God also meant that God, victorious over the evil powers, was coming to establish his rule of justice and love. Paul seems to avoid the Reign-of-God terminology. The term appears rarely in his epistles (Rom. 14:17; 1 Cor. 4:20; 6:9–10; 15:24, 50; Gal. 5:21; 1 Thess. 2:12). Young Saul had not been a companion of the Galilean. He did not belong to the milieu that gathered the logia of the Lord and pondered over them. He perceived the victory of God's Reign through the person of the Risen One. He saw the glory of God "on the face of Christ." He perceived the power of the Spirit in what it did to Jesus the Lord. The person of the Crucified and Risen One incarnates all that the coming of God in his glory could imply. In other words, when Paul speaks of "power of the Resurrection," of triumph of "glory" over "dishonor," of "power" over "weakness" (1 Cor. 15:42–43), he speaks, in equivalent terms, of the Reign of God, of the victory of God's love over all powers. This is what he means when he exclaims: "thanks be to God, who gives us the victory through our Lord Jesus Christ" (1 Cor. 15:57).

No doubt there is a difference of connotation between the Reign of God in the Gospels and the new life in the Spirit in Paul. In the Gospels, the reign is spelled out through the narrative of what Jesus "said and did" (Acts 1:1), whereas, for Paul, the outlook is concentrated on the death and the Resurrection. The image gains in intensity what it loses in precision. But the Pauline "gospel of Jesus Christ" does not differ essentially from the Good News of the Kingdom in the gospels. It does not reduce Christ to a hieratic symbol, like other deities. "Every knee in heaven, on earth and under the earth," is not invited to bow to a lifeless object of worship but to the Servant whose death on the cross was the proof that God loves us (Rom. 5:8) and whose exaltation manifested the ultimate power of this love.

Power of Salvation

It is the gospel itself that gives power to the apostolic mission. "I am not ashamed of the gospel, for it is the power of God for salvation to everyone who believes, to the Jew first and also to the Greek" (Rom. 1:16). When saying "I am not ashamed of the gospel," the former student of the Tarsus college uses the rhetorical figure of litotes, which consists in saying less to mean more. Shunning "lofty speech and wisdom," his "speech and message were not in plausible words of wisdom, but in demonstration of the Spirit and of power" (1 Cor. 2:4).

The Good News is the "power of God unto salvation," first because it is the Good News *of God*, endowed with divine authority and energy. "Word of God" (1 Thess. 2:13; Phil. 1:14) has the force poetically described by Isaiah:

> As the rain and the snow come down from heaven
> and do not return there but water the earth,
> making it bring forth and sprout,
> giving seed to the sower and bread to the eater,

so shall my word be that goes out from my mouth.
It shall not return to me empty,
but it shall accomplish that which I purpose,
and shall succeed in the thing for which I sent it.

(Isa. 55:10–11)

More precisely, the Good News is power as the Good News *of
Jesus Christ.* The gospel makes Jesus Christ and what he signifies to be present in the world. For those who receive it, it conveys
the impact of the Damascus encounter and the upheaval it produced in Paul. Those whom it reaches receive "the revelation of
the glory of God on the face of Christ." Through the gospel, the
meeting with the Risen One sways the whole world. God himself,
in Christ, makes his love present in the world and undertakes
universal reconciliation (cf. 2 Cor. 5:19).

Good News *of God,* Good News *of Jesus Christ,* the gospel
is Good News "concerning his Son," which finds expression in
the person of "Our Lord Jesus Christ." It is the news of the final
triumph of divine love which, in the flesh of Jesus, has assumed
all the human frailty and, in the Spirit, has brought to this sinful and deadly flesh the life and power of a new life and of a
new world.

The Gospel Day by Day

As seen above, Paul uses the noun "gospel" more often than the
verb "evangelize." Indeed, he does evangelize. But continuously
and more frequently he returns to what animates his activity, the
inherent power of the gospel.

In the Acts of the Apostles, the proportion is reversed. The
word "gospel" is used only twice (15:7; 20:24). On the contrary,
the verb "evangelize" occurs fifteen times. This disproportion
was greater still in the Gospel of Luke, where the word "gospel"
is totally absent whereas the verb "evangelize" occurs ten times.[6]

---

6. It is the opposite in Mark which does use the verb and has the noun
ten times. Mark is more "Pauline" than Luke.

Paul goes to the heart of the gospel, "power of salvation," by itself. Luke, for Jesus as for the apostles, becomes the historian of the gospel and traces the way followed by the agents of the gospel. However, it would be wrong to conclude that Luke gave way to triumphalist activism as if he had been a kind of Pelagian missiologist. In Acts, it is the theme of the Word, the *logos*, that plays the role of dynamic focus of evangelizing action. It is the Word that leads to faith (Acts 4:4; 8:25; 10:44; 11:1; 13:7, 48; 15:7; 17:11). It belongs to the essence of apostolic identity (6:24) and sustains the courage of missionaries (4:29, 31). It is identified with the mission of the church since the growth of the Word is equated with the growth of the church (6:7; 12:24; 20:32). This shift of terminology is puzzling. Can we suppose that, one or two generations after Paul, by the time Luke wrote his work, the word "gospel" had begun losing its force and that recourse had to be made to the hallowed theme of the Word, of sound biblical parentage, in order to express the power of the message?

One or two generations after Paul, as years were going on, the need was felt to spell out the reception of the message in terms of daily life, day after day, in the context of the household and of society. One cannot live in a condition of on-going ecstasy. Good News must be received keeping our feet on the ground. The Jewish communities of the Diaspora had found a *modus vivendi* amid the surrounding pagan world. Taking inspiration from this model, the post-Pauline letters set up household codes regulating relationships between elders and the youth, husband and wife, masters and slaves as well since slaves were part of the household (Titus 2:1–10; cf. Col. 3:18–4:1; Eph. 5:22–6:9; 1 Pet. 2:18–3:7). The communities also had to be organized (1 Tim. 3:1–13; Titus 1:5–9) and cautioned against troublemakers (1 Tim. 1:19–20; 6:3–10; 2 Tim. 2:16–18; 3:1–9; 4:3–5; Titus 1:10–16; 3:9–11). A style of life was advocated, "peaceful and quiet, godly and dignified in every way" (1 Tim. 2:2), "without anger and quarreling" for men, in "modesty and self-control" for women (1 Tim. 2:8–10; Titus 3:1–3). Women are invited to be busy in good works. For widows particularly, a detailed program is proposed (1 Tim.

5:1–16). The proclamation of the Good News or *kerygma* leads to exhortation or *parenesis*. The shift goes back to Paul himself who did not only evoke the "transformation into the image of the glory of God" (2 Cor. 3:18) but articulated this "transformation" in detailed contrasting lists of "fruits of the flesh" and "fruits of the Spirit" (Gal. 5:19–25).

After Paul it was necessary to continue this translation of the Good News in terms of works and days as time went on. It would be unfair to qualify this movement as banalization. In fact, it amounted to an incarnation of the message. Post-Pauline generations were still imbued with the spirit of the Good News. They continued to adopt the old faith confession taught by the Apostle: "Remember Jesus Christ, risen from the dead, the offspring of David, as preached in my gospel" (2 Tim. 2:8). They continue to commune with "the appearing of our Savior Christ Jesus, who abolished death and brought life and immortality to light through the gospel" (2 Tim. 1:10).

PART TWO

The Mission

"Called to be an apostle, set apart for the gospel of God,"
the messenger starts his mission. Will he move at random
or will he follow a master plan? Does his mission address
the whole world or a specific field? Which methods will
he use? We could speak of global strategy and local tac-
tics. But this military language would not suit the spiritual
depth of the Apostle's path.

6

The Project of Paul: The People of the New Covenant

Sent to announce the gospel, will the Apostle go to the world pushed about by the wind or by the Spirit, hunting for souls to be saved as he chances to meet them? Did he preach the gospel like the wandering philosophers of those days? Or, on the contrary, moved by the holy ambition to convert the world, did he plan his campaigns, pointing out on a map the economic and cultural centers from where the light of the gospel would spread all over the world? In technical terms, it is the question of a Pauline mission paradigm. But the word "paradigm" suggests a set framework which, from the outset, would have encompassed the activity of the Apostle. The word "project" is preferable to qualify an approach which, following a main line, became clearer progressively, under the guidance of the Spirit, as conditions developed. Such is the question: When Paul went to the nations, did he sow the gospel indiscriminately or was he guided by a set project? We could say that he had no other project than the divine project and that he entrusted his work to the mind of God. But precisely, how did he perceive the mind of God as regards the world of the "nations"?

Religious and Philosophical Propaganda

The Mediterranean world knew various types of ideological and religious propaganda. One might be tempted to view Paul's apostolate as one or the other of those types. Is the comparison convincing?

Missionary Judaism?

Can the zeal of Paul be considered as a variant of a missionary dynamism that would have characterized Judaism in those days? Paul, the Pharisee who had become a disciple of Jesus Christ, would have just applied to his new faith the missionary zeal which already animated the Jewish world.

It is a fact that, through the Diaspora, faith in the God of Israel spread remarkably in the Greco-Roman world. We have seen above the spread of this Diaspora to Rome, Alexandria, Antioch, and beyond the Euphrates. Was this growth due to a missionary drive in Judaism? The question is disputed. Some authors deny any form of Jewish proselytism.[1] To a good extent the answer depends on what we mean by "mission" and "missionary." There was certainly no organized and systematic Jewish endeavor to win the pagan world over to Judaism. Obviously, the Jerusalem Sanhedrin had no *Congregatio de Propaganda Fide*. Neither had Judaism established a Society for Foreign Missions. However, the expansion of Judaism is also a fact. Jewish faith was at the same time disturbing and attractive. Its monotheism, its

---

1. See discussion in B. G. Bamberger, *Proselytism in the Talmudic Period* (New York: Hebrew University Press), 1939; reprint New York: Ktav, 1968); É. Will and C. Orrieux, *Prosélytisme Juif? Histoire d'une erreur* (Paris: Belles Lettres, 1992); C. H. Bedell, "Mission in Intertestamental Judaism," in W. J. Larkin and J. F. Williams (eds.), *Mission in the New Testament* (New York: Orbis Books, 1998), 21–29; P. W. Barnett, "Jewish Mission in the Era of the New Testament and the Apostle Paul," in P. Bolt and M. Thompson (eds.), *The Gospel to the Nations: Perspectives on Paul's Mission* (Leicester: Apollos, 2000), 263–81; J. C. Paget, "Jewish Proselytism at the Time of Christian Origins," *JSNT* 62 (1996), 65–103; J. P. Lemonon, "Le Judaïsme avait-il une pensée et une pratique missionnaire au début de notre ère ?" in ACFEB, *Le Judaïsme à l'aube de l'ère chrétienne* (LD 186; Paris: Cerf, 2001), 299–329; F. Blanchetière, *Les premiers chrétiens étaient-ils missionnaires? (30–135)* (Paris: Cerf, 2002).

precise and demanding ethic, and its community spirit exercised a power of attraction. Many sympathizers admired and observed the *Torah* while remaining "proselytes of the gate." Many also, individually or collectively, embraced integral Judaism, including circumcision. Members of the Diaspora did not hesitate to bear witness to their faith. The case of the conversion of the kingdom of Abiadene is significant. This kingdom was situated in Upper Mesopotamia, and its capital was Arbela (presently Erbil). In the first century CE, it formed a buffer state between the Parthian Empire and the *limes* of the Roman Empire. Before he became a king, young prince Izates met a Jewish merchant called Ananias, under whose influence he converted to Judaism. At the same time, his mother, Hellen, had followed a similar way. When Izates became a king, his mother and Ananias, fearing hostile reactions from the population, advised him not to go to the extent of being circumcised. They alleged that observing the Law is more important than the ritual of circumcision. But another Jew from Galilee, called Eleazar, more zealous, reversed the argument. It is not enough to study the Law, he said; it has to be observed. He convinced the young king, who underwent circumcision, became a full Jew, and made his people a Jewish people.[2] He became famous for his generosity to the temple and to people of Jerusalem on the occasion of a famine.[3] All this took place between 36 and 60 CE, at the same time as Paul's ministry.

This is a typical case of the dynamism of the Diaspora. Without missionary structure, it grew through witness of faith and life, by means of social, political, and commercial networks belonging to ordinary daily life. Issued from the Diaspora, Paul inherited its

---

2. According to É. Will and C. Orrieux, the conversion movement did not extend to the people and remained limited to the circle of the royal family (p. 194). Actually, Josephus makes no mention of a mass conversion. But, in the mentality of those days, it went without saying. It is unthinkable that the Abiadene dynasty could have engaged the caritative and sumptuary expenses in Jerusalem at the expense of the royal treasury without the support of public opinion.

3. According to Josephus, *AntJud* 20.17–53.

dynamism and used its networks. Yet a major difference subsists. The Diaspora witness is collective and mostly anonymous. There is no example of an individual "Jewish missionary." So, the case of Paul remains specific. He is a particular individual "set apart from the womb of [his] mother and called by his grace" (Gal. 1:13) to be an "apostle set apart to announce the gospel of God" (Rom. 1:1). The mission of Paul cannot be reduced to a particular case of the dynamism shown by the Jewish Diaspora.

Itinerant Philosophical Propaganda

Though the citizen of Greco-Roman cities would not have met any Jewish itinerant missionary, he would have come across another form of proselytism, that of itinerant philosophers who drifted from town to town and from country to country to spread their views on the world and on life.[4] The campaigns of Alexander and the reigns of his successors, the Diadochi, had opened the mental boundaries of the Mediterranean world. There followed a flurry of interreligious and ideological exchange, carried collectively by populations on the move and also by colorful figures who spread new cults and new ideas. A typical and almost mythical example is that of Apollonius (16–97 CE) from Tyana in Cappadocia. His life has been reported by Philostratus in the third century CE. A Pythagorean philosopher, belonging like Paul to the first century and therefore his contemporary, Apollonius is credited with thaumaturgic powers. He is even reported to have brought back to life a girl who had died at the time of marriage. Like Paul, he traveled, and his journeys took him from Cilicia to Antioch, Nineveh, Babylon, as far as India from where he returned to Athens, Alexandria, and Rome. Since Philostratus wrote his account two centuries after the events, it is difficult to sort out the part of history and of imagination. Anyway, the story is an illustration of the typology of an itinerant philosopher going from town to town spreading his ideas. Already in the third cen-

---

4. Cf. L. J. Lietaert Peerbole, *Paul the Missionary* (CBET 34; Leuven: Peeters, 2003), 55–79.

tury BCE, Diogenes the Cynic had been another example of an itinerant philosopher. He presented an image of integral liberty; defying all social conventions, he carried this image from Sinope on the Black Sea, his birthplace, to Athens, Corinth, Samothrace, and all over Greece.

Eastern Cults

At the same time and in the same way, the cults of Eastern deities spread all over the Greco-Roman world. From Egypt came the cult of Isis and Serapis and from Persia that of Mithra. Aesculapius, the healing god, was particularly popular. His temple, the *asklepion*, was originally found in Epidaurus in Greece. Later on, it was reproduced at Pergamon, in Asia Minor, Athens in Greece, in Rome, and in other places. There also, the spread of this cult was not due to organized propaganda. It was a spontaneous development through socio-economic or familial networks. The mobility of Roman legions and of their veterans facilitated the spread of these cults. But a great difference remains between these small, clannish groups, confined to their rites of initiation, and the universalistic movement of Paul which embraced all the dimensions of the divine plan on humanity.

In this connection, it may not be out of point to refer to the encounter between the West and the Indian world. The exchange of ideas had extended to India. It worked both ways. Eastward, the Greco-Buddhist art of Gandhara in India, which developed toward the beginnings of the Christian era, merged Indian and Greek arts. On the other side, there was the case of Democritus of Miletus, a disciple of Anaxagoras and Leucippus, who had gone to Egypt to learn geometry from priests, to Persia to learn from the Chaldeans, and who had been associated with the gymnosophists of India.[5]

Buddhism especially had begun reaching the West. Actually, at that time, it would have been Buddhism that provided the clear-

---

5. Diogenes Laertius, *Life and Opinions of Eminent Philosophers* 9.7.

est example of missionary dynamism and systematic religious propaganda. Such were the Buddha's instructions to his disciples:

> Go ye forth, O Bhikkus,
> for the good of the many, for the welfare of the many,
> out of compassion for the world,
> teach the Dhamma
> that is beautiful in the beginning, middle and end,
> expound both the spirit and the letter of the holy life
> completely fulfilled, perfectly pure.[6]

Later on, the Emperor Asoka (268–232 BCE) became a fervent propagandist of Buddhism. He sent nine missionaries all over India, but also to Sri Lanka, Myanmar, and Thailand. One of them, Maharakkhita, was even sent to "Yona," that is Greece. We do not know whether he reached it. But the fact that he was sent reveals the bridge that connected East and West. Hinduism followed up. Philo reports that he met "gymnosophists" in Alexandria.[7] The Greek historian Strabo reports that a philosopher, who was a member of an embassy sent from India to Rome, set fire to himself in the center of Athens: "the gymnosophist, anointed with oil and wearing only a loin cloth, climbed the pyre smiling." The city of Athens erected a tomb bearing the inscription: "Here lies Zarmanochegas, an Indian, native of Bargosa, who died of voluntary death according to his ancestral customs."[8] But these were only exceptional events. Even if Paul heard of it, which is quite doubtful, he would not have been tempted to imitate them.

---

6. *Mahāvagga* 1.11.1, "the propaganda or the gift of the Law (*dharmadāna*) is a duty which Buddhism enjoins to its adepts, as witnessed by the inscriptions of Asoka and, in the Great Vehicle, the traditional formulas which conclude *sutras*, formulas which score the merits acquired by spreading the sacred texts" (J. Filiozat, "Le Bouddhisme," in *L'Inde classique: Manuel d'études indiennes* [ed. L. Renou and J. Filiozat; Paris: École Française d'Extrême Orient, 1953], 3:409).

7. Philo, *Prob.* 11. It could have been Jain *digambara* monks. Cf. L. Legrand, *The Bible on Cultures* (New York: Orbis Books, 2001), 154–55.

8. Strabo, *Geographia* 15.73.

Intercultural and interreligious sharing between East and West worked both ways. The gold, incense, and myrrh of the Magi symbolize this exchange. The Acts gives an ironical image of the open-mindedness of those days: "all the Athenians and the foreigners who lived there would spend their time in nothing except telling or hearing something new" (Acts 17:21). Paul derides this ill-minded syncretism: Athenians went to the extent of taking "Resurrection" (*anastasis*) as the consort goddess of Jesus (Acts 17:18). In such a setting, Paul could easily have been mistaken as another peddler of a new-fangled wisdom or of a strange cult. To some extent, he could even take advantage of this intellectual excitement.

But Paul intends to keep away from this trend. His is not a message of wisdom but of the folly of a crucified Messiah. From a superficial viewpoint, his action might appear to be that of an itinerant preacher. But his internal motivation and the aim he has in mind have nothing to do with those who parade "lofty speech" or wisdom: "for I decided to know nothing among you except Jesus Christ and him crucified." And he explains: "my speech and my message were not in plausible words of wisdom, but in demonstration of the Spirit and of power, that your faith might not rest in the wisdom of men but in the power of God" (1 Cor. 2:1–4). He viewed himself as a "steward of the mystery of God" (1 Cor. 4:1). What was then this "mystery of God" that he announced? Which perspective on the divine plan was opened by the revelation of a crucified Messiah?

The People of the New Covenant

Paul is not the propagandist of a new ideology or of another religion. He is the messenger of the Good News, and the Good News is addressed to a people, the People of the Promises and of the Covenant. As Cerfaux puts it at the beginning of his *Theology of the Church according to Saint Paul*, a book that had a great influence on the orientations of Vatican II: "We consider that the theology of Saint Paul did not make a clean sweep of the Jewish views. It assimilated them when they fitted the Christian synthe-

sis. As the starting point of the theology of the Church we posit
the theology of the 'People of God.'"⁹ The same can be said of
the "theology of mission" that guided the Apostle. The "People
of God" is the focus of his project. His mission strategy did not
consist in accumulating individual conversions but in gathering
the People of God in response to the gospel, while redefining the
identity of the Chosen People in the light of the Resurrection. He
develops the point especially in Romans 9–11.¹⁰

The People of God

Paul begins expressing his visceral attachment to his "brothers
according to the flesh" (Rom. 9:2–5; cf. Rom. 11:1; Gal. 2:15; Phil.
3:5–6; cf. Acts 21:39; 22:3; 23:5; 26:5). Many failed to respond
to the Good News. But God, in his sovereign liberty, has called
the nations and in them was accomplished the prophecy of Hosea

9. L. Cerfaux, *La théologie de l'église suivant Saint Paul, Nouvelle
Édition* (Unam Sanctam 54; Paris: Cerf, 1965), 13. The first edition went
back to 1942. Cerfaux was a precursor. At that time, the tendency was to
see Paul as opposing Judaism. There is now general agreement to recognize a greater continuity between Judaism and Paul's thought. This *New
Perspective on Paul* originated with an important article of K. Stendahl,
"The Apostle Paul and the Introspective Conscience of the West," *HTR* 56
(1963): 199–215. Cf. E. P. Sanders, *Paul and Palestinian Judaism* (London:
SCM Press, 1977), 1–12; C. Tassin, "Paul dans le monde Juif du Ier siècle,"
in *Paul de Tarse* (ed. J. Schlosser; LD 165; Paris: Cerf, 1996), 171–93.

10. It would exceed the limits of this study to review all the problems
raised by these chapters. The bibliography is considerable: cf. S. Légasse,
L'épître de Paul aux Romains (LD Com 10; Paris: Cerf, 2002), 567–72. In
addition to the many exegetical problems raised by the text, a basic question concerns the connection between these chapters and the rest of the
epistle. Cf. J.-N. Aletti, *Comment Dieu est-il juste? Clefs pour interpréter
l'épître de Paul aux Romains* (Paris: Seuil, 1991), 125–203. Our purpose is
only to point out the mission strategy revealed by the text. The title given
by Aletti to this section is quite to the point: "Israel and the Nations." It is
not only "the question of Israel" as considered by many studies. It is also
the question of the nations. The chapters do not treat only of the perennity
of the vocation of Israel. They also consider the new dimension and new
identity which the nations bring to Israel.

2:25: "'Those who were not my people I will call 'my people,' and her who was not beloved I will call 'beloved.' And in the very place where it was said to them, 'You are not my people,' there they will be called 'sons of the living God'" (Rom. 9:25–26). The divine plan was that the admission of the pagans should stir the jealousy of Israel and incite it to accept salvation (Rom. 11:11, 14).

> So I ask, did they stumble in order that they might fall? By no means! Rather through their trespass salvation has come to the Gentiles, so as to make Israel jealous. Now if their trespass means riches for the world, and if their failure means riches for the Gentiles, how much more will their full inclusion mean! Now I am speaking to you Gentiles. Inasmuch then as I am an apostle to the Gentiles, I magnify my ministry in order somehow to make my fellow Jews jealous, and thus save some of them. For if their rejection means the reconciliation of the world, what will their acceptance mean but life from the dead? (Rom. 11:11–15)

It is a mysterious divine strategy that Paul tries to decipher so as to become its agent. The mainstream remains "those of his own blood," the people of Israel, since "the gifts and the calling of God are irrevocable" (Rom. 11:29). The nations constitute the mass of maneuver, but the final aim is that "all Israel may be saved" (Rom. 11:26). The divine plan remains focused on the people of Abraham. Cerfaux notes that Paul avoids using the phrase "new people" to preserve "the continuity of the divine work and the perennity of the privilege granted to the Chosen People."[11] Paul reminds the Christians of pagan origin that they are

> a wild olive shoot grafted in among the others and now sharing in the nourishing root of the olive tree. . . . Remember it is not you who support the root, but the root that supports you. . . . You were cut from what is by nature a wild olive tree, and grafted, contrary to nature, into a cultivated olive tree. (Rom. 11:17–18, 24)

---

11. L. Cerfaux, *La théologie de l'église*, 60.

There is only one trunk and one root. The nations will not be an addition to the Chosen People as if they were another people; neither will they substitute for it. "Has God rejected his people?" asks Paul, and he answers: "By no means! For I myself am an Israelite, a descendant of Abraham, a member of the tribe of Benjamin. God has not rejected his people whom he foreknew." And he quotes the episode when Elijah complained to God to be the only one left to believe in him. "But what is God's reply to him? 'I have kept for myself seven thousand men who have not bowed the knee to Baal.' So too at the present time there is a remnant, chosen by grace" (Rom. 11:1–5). Many branches have been cut, but the olive tree stands and even the branches which have been cut off could be grafted again on the old trunk (Rom. 11:23–24). One can but trust and admire "the depth of the riches and wisdom and knowledge of God! How unsearchable are his judgments and how inscrutable his ways!" (Rom. 11:33).

The Mystery of Israel

The Pauline mission is rooted in the election of Israel. Is this standpoint still relevant for us today? Is the mystery still a challenge for us?

Already in the beginning of the second century CE, Marcion intended to expurgate the Bible from the Old Testament, alleged to be the voice of a vengeful God, the antithesis of the God of love of the New Testament. He was condemned, and the Old Testament was acknowledged as an integral part of the Christian Bible. However, a kind of covert Marcionism has been lingering among Christians. In the course of history, it led to antisemitism which culminated in the horrors of the Shoah. The study of Paul and of the New Testament in general invites us to question the practical Marcionism that subsists in an attitude of uneasiness and neglect toward the Old Testament.

Cut from its roots, the Christian message loses its force and contents. As Pope John Paul II said, "Meditating on the mystery of Israel and its 'irreversible call' Christians explore the mystery of their own roots. In its biblical sources which they share with their Jewish brethren, they find the indispensable elements to feed their faith and deepen it."[12]

A typical instance can be found in a fundamental point of Christian faith, the first article of the Creed: "I believe in God the Father." Faith in God the Father turns into vague sentimentalism if, with the Old Testament, we do not realize that the One we dare call "Father" is primarily God the Creator, the Infinite, the Eternal, the Thrice Holy. He is the one whom Jesus enables us to call "Father." When Jesus the Jew says, "When you pray, say 'Abba, Father,'" he says it through the vision of Isaiah in the Temple: "'Holy, holy, holy is the Lord of hosts; the whole earth is full of his glory!' . . . And I said: 'Woe is me! For I am lost; for I am a man of unclean lips, and I dwell in the midst of a people of unclean lips; for my eyes have seen the King, the Lord of hosts!'" (Isa. 6:3–5). Then only will the words of Jesus move our hearts as the expression of the infinite gift bestowed upon us.

The New Covenant

But the People of God, even though not a new people insofar as it is the one and single People of God, is a people which, in its faith in the Risen Christ, lives now in the "newness of the Spirit" (Rom. 7:6). Prophets had announced that days would come when God "would make a new covenant," which he would write in the hearts (Jer. 31:31–33); it would be the covenant according to the Spirit (Ezek. 36:25–28; Isa. 59:21), the "eternal covenant" (Isa. 55:3; 61:8). These days have come: now the "Israel of God" (Gal. 6:16) lives according to the "new covenant" (1 Cor. 11:25; 2 Cor. 3:6), according to the Spirit (Rom. 8:13–17; 2 Cor. 3:14–17; Gal. 5:16–18, 22, 25), filled with the "love of God poured in our hearts by the Spirit given to us" (Rom. 5:5). The new times have arrived: "if anyone is in Christ, he is a new creation. The old has passed away; behold, the new has come" (2 Cor. 5:17). Baptism, participation through faith in the death and Resurrection of Christ, incorporates the believer in the new life (Rom. 6:4).

---

12. General Audience of April 28, 1999.

Since the People of God is no longer defined by lineage "according to the flesh" but by "the Spirit of the Lord," it follows that belonging to this People of God is no longer restricted to ethnic descent. "It is those of faith who are the sons of Abraham. . . . Those who are of faith are blessed along with Abraham, the man of faith" (Gal. 3:7, 9). This is illustrated by the allegory of the two children of Abraham. Ishmael, born from the slave according to the flesh, represents those who are under the slavery of the Law. Isaac, born of the free woman, according to the Spirit stands for the people gathered in the "Jerusalem above" (Gal. 4:22–26). Paul draws the same significance in the election of Jacob against Esau:

> Not all who are descended from Israel belong to Israel, and not all are children of Abraham because they are his off-spring, but "Through Isaac shall your offspring be named." This means that it is not the children of the flesh who are the children of God, but the children of the promise are counted as offspring. (Rom. 9:6–8)

So now the door is open to those whose "circumcision is a matter of the heart, by the Spirit, not by letter" (Rom. 2:29).

Israel was called to be a "light to the nations so that salvation may reach the ends of the earth" (Isa. 42:6; 49:6). The election of Israel was to extend to all the people of the earth (Ps. 87; Isa. 2:3; 14:10; 19:21, 24–25; 25:6–8; 60:2–3; Zech. 8:20–22). For Paul, the Resurrection of the Messiah signifies that the hour has come when, on the basis of faith and not of the Law, of the Spirit and not of the flesh, the promises and the covenant were to take their universal dimensions.

A New Identity

It is the new identity that Paul will propose to his Jewish brothers and open to the Gentiles. This identity must be viewed in the pluralistic context of Judaism prior to the destruction of the Temple in 70 CE. At the time of Paul and of Jesus, there were several forms of Jewish consciousness. For the Sadducees, members of the priestly aristocracy of Jerusalem, the focus of Jewish identity was the Temple and its cult. Scribes and Pharisees laid the stress on the Law, studied and observed. For the Zealots, faith in the promises was attached to the land, the *eretz Israel*, for which they were soon going to fight and give their life. The Qumran group kept itself apart on the shores of the Dead Sea to shun any compromise with Belial. On the other hand, the Diaspora Jews had to meet the pagan world, and differences were not lacking between Alexandrian and Antiochian tendencies, as well as in the various positions adopted to oppose or to reconcile Moses and Greek wisdom and Egyptian science.[13] Not to speak of the Samaritans who, in their own way, considered themselves as the true disciples of Moses. The Pauline project must be viewed in the context of those various forms of Jewish awareness. It presents a double characteristic.

It is situated within Judaism. It intends to belong to the quest of identity, to the search for the meaning of the promises and of the covenant, which agitated the Jewish world round the beginnings of the Christian era. On the other hand, it proposed a principle of identity that upset the established opinions radically. The identity of Israel was no longer to be found in belonging to Israel "according to the flesh" since "not all who descended from Israel belong to Israel" (Rom. 9:6). Neither was this identity found in the Law since "the Law of the Spirit of life in Christ Jesus has set me free from the law of sin and death" (Rom. 8:2). Or again, it was not the cult of the Temple that defined the People of God since "your body is the temple of the Holy Spirit within you whom you have from God" (1 Cor. 6:19). The sign of belonging to the lineage of Abraham is no longer circumcision since "neither circumcision counts nor uncircumcision, but a new creation" (Gal. 6:15). It is faith in Christ which now gives its identity to the People of the New Covenant, the faith that consists in "knowing him and the power of his Resurrection, sharing his sufferings" (Phil. 3:10).

---

13. Cf. L. Legrand, *The Bible on Cultures* (New York: Orbis Books, 2000), 52–60.

Paul's Jewish brethren were understandably upset by this radical questioning. He is aware of it: a crucified Messiah is a scandal for the Jews (1 Cor. 1:25). For them, Paul was a heretic. But he was not a renegade. For Paul, on the contrary, the gospel is the manifestation of "the power and wisdom of God" (1 Cor. 1:24), the revelation of the "mystery" (Rom. 11:25, 33–35) of God's plan for his people. Such was the aim intended by God and therefore the main line of the Pauline project. It is an asymptotic perspective. Its realization belongs to the unfathomable wisdom of God. But it commands the mission policy of the Apostle, the guiding line of his mission strategy.

It was only in the course of time, through the experience of his life and of the ups and downs of his ministry that the Apostle will be able to articulate his orientations, specify his aims, and perceive more and more deeply the implications of his encounter with the Risen One. The outcome will be the outline given in Galatians and the synthesis offered in Romans. He would not have perceived straightaway all these implications. Yet, it was this illuminating and upsetting encounter that led Saul the Pharisee to reverse his sense of Jewish identity and open it to the nations.

The *Ekklēsia*

The divine economy and consequently the mission strategy of Paul embrace the collective dimensions of the People of God. Images are not lacking to express this communitarian aspect: orchard (1 Cor. 3:6–9; Rom. 11:17–21); building (2 Cor. 10:8), temple (1 Cor. 3:10–17; 6:19), city (Phil. 3:20), and especially Jerusalem (Rom. 9:33; Gal. 4:25–26), household (2 Cor. 5:1–2; Phlm. 4), and family with its paternal and fraternal relationships. The image of the body, in connection with the body of the Risen Lord, is particularly noteworthy (Rom. 12:4–5; 1 Cor. 12:22–27): the bibliography is copious.

But, for Paul, it is mostly the theme of the church, of the *ekklēsia*, that expresses this communitarian aspect.[14] The word

---

14. Here again a problem of translation arises. *Ekklēsia* means "church"

ekklēsia appears with an exceptional frequency.[15] In general, as against the Pastoral Epistles (1–2 Timothy and Titus), the letters are addressed to *ekklēsiai* (1 Cor. 1:2; 2 Cor. 1:2; Gal. 1:2; 1 Thess. 1:1; cf. 2 Thess. 1:1; Col. 1:2).[16]

The use of the word probably precedes Paul. It was the term used by the Jerusalem community. The witness of Acts (5:11; 8:13; 11:22; 12:1; 15:4, 22) is confirmed by Paul himself when he confesses repeatedly that he has "persecuted the *ekklēsia*" (1 Cor. 15:9; Gal. 1:13; Phil. 3:6). However, he made it a technical term to qualify the communities gathered by the Good News. The word summarizes the ultimate purpose of his mission endeavor. It aims at establishing *ekklēsiai* gathered by the gospel. Several converging reasons of different importance explain the choice of this word.

In the Hellenistic world, the *ekklēsia* referred to the assembly of the citizens gathered to discuss questions of general interest and to come to a resolution. This does not mean that Paul considered it as a model to be followed in the believing community since, anyway, the Hellenistic *ekklēsia* was not particularly concerned with religious problems. However, as a missionary endowed with an inborn gift for communication, Paul perceived the interest of a word that evoked a gathering of free and responsible members of a community.

---

evidently. But, in the course of history, the word "church" has taken institutional and even clerical connotations, favored or rejected according to theological and confessional tendencies. Renan's word is well known: "Jesus preached the Kingdom and what happened was the Church." The irony conveys the bitterness which the word evokes in certain contexts. In general, we shall keep to the Greek word *ekklēsia*, which brings us back to what it meant for the Apostle before it started its semantic course in history.

15. Out of the 144 times it occurs in the entire New Testament, it figures 44 times in the authentic Pauline letters. If we add the 16 times it is found in the other letters attributed to Paul and 23 times in Acts, we get in Pauline circles a total of 83 or ¾ of the total New Testament use.

16. Phil 1:1 has an equivalent address to the structures of *episcopoi* and *diakonoi*. The only exceptions are the short note to Philemon, which is a personal message, and the epistle to Romans addressed to a community of which he is not the founder and the structure of which is not well known to him.

But this was not the essential point. For Paul the Jew, the word came mostly from the Scriptures and from his Israelite inheritance. The word *ekklēsia* came from the Greek translation of the Bible, the Septuagint commonly used in the Diaspora. It rendered the Hebrew *qahal* (gathering, assembly). It referred to the gathering of the People of God at the foot on Mount Sinai to enter into alliance with the Lord (Deut. 4:10; 9:10), to recall it in the plains of Moab (Deut. 31:30), at the entrance to the Holy Land (Josh. 8:35), during its conquest (Josh. 20:2), and at the renewal of the Alliance on the return from the Babylonian Exile (Ezra 2:64; Neh. 7:66; 8:2). It was again the *qahal* that gathered in the Temple on the occasion of the functions held to commemorate the Sinai commitment (Deut. 23; Ps. 22:23, 26; 35:18; 40:10; 149:1). Joel 2:15–17 gives a picturesque description of the ritual of the *qahal*. Called at the sound of the horn, people gathered in the Temple, observing collectively fasting and continence. The position of priests is indicated "between the vestibule and the altar," where they start singing the lamentation, which people will resume together. By applying this word *ekklēsia* to communities founded among the nations, Paul highlighted their continuity with the Israelite covenant.

The word *ekklēsia* also evokes the theme of the election, of the call of the people especially called (*klētos* in Greek) by God for a specific vocation (*klēsis* in Greek):

> You are a people holy to the Lord your God. The Lord your God has chosen you to be a people for his treasured possession, out of all the peoples who are on the face of the earth. It was not because you were more in number than any other people that the Lord set his love on you and chose you, for you were the fewest of all peoples, but it is because the Lord loves you and is keeping the oath that he swore to your fathers, that the Lord has brought you out with a mighty hand and redeemed you from the house of slavery, from the hand of Pharaoh king of Egypt. (Deut. 7:6–8; cf. 4:20; 10:15; 14:2; 32:8–12)

Now, at the end of times, all the nations receive the call to election, to be "a kingdom of priests, a holy people" (Exod. 19:6). When Paul calls the Christians of Rome "called of Jesus Christ, called to be saints, loved by God" (Rom. 1:6–7), he does not suggest that the disciples of Jesus would have acquired a high level of moral perfection. He applies to them the terms of the election of Israel. He considers them as a full-fledged *ekklēsia*, a community called to be God's "treasured possession because the Lord set his love on them and chose them." So he urges them to fulfill their mission as a "kingdom of priests:" "I appeal to you therefore, brothers, by the mercies of God, to present your bodies as a living sacrifice, holy and acceptable to God, which is your spiritual worship" (Rom. 12:1). Once gathered by the Sinai covenant and the Temple of Jerusalem, the "kingdom of priests," the "holy nation," is now found gathered by faith in Jesus Christ in Ephesus, Corinth, Rome, and even in Spain (Rom. 15:28), the *finis terrae*, the end of the earth. Right in the midst of the pagan world of Corinth and Rome, the *ekklēsia* of the nations carried the divine aura that once shone on Sinai, partook of the sanctity of Jerusalem, and was called to diffuse its radiance.

The Greco-Roman world knew a multiple variety of associations, select groups, and fraternities. Romans had their *collegia*, associations based on professional or commercial affinities. Greeks had *thiasoi*, the religiosity of which could find ebullient expressions. Closer to the Christian mind were the words *koinōnia* (community, communion) and *adelphotēs* brotherhood (cf. 1 Pet. 2:17; 5:9). The word *synagogē* did not apply only to Jewish "synagogues." It could be used for any gathering, as in Acts 13:43. As witnessed by James 2:2, it could also apply to the Christian community; it is indeed semantically close to *ekklēsia*. Paul chose the word *ekklēsia*. His option was meaningful. By applying the word to the Christians of Thessalonica, Philippi, Corinth, he showed the purpose that his apostolate intended. It was "that in Christ Jesus the blessing of Abraham might come to the Gentiles, so that we might receive the promised Spirit through faith" (Gal. 3:14).

A Small Remnant

"To the nations" (Gal. 2:9): such was the vast program that the Apostle followed "from Jerusalem and all the way around to Illyricum" (Rom. 15:19), on the Adriatic coast, before proceeding to Rome, which he intends to be a basis for a drive to Spain. There, he would reach the Pillars of Hercules, the western end of the then-known world. We shall return later to this western vision of the world. Presently we note that this geographical setting was covered by Paul only in a scattered smattering of dotted lines.

First, he covered only cities. His ministry was basically urban, leaving out all the rural hinterland. Even the cities that he evangelized constitute only a small selection of the vast urban landscape of the Roman Empire. Moreover the Pauline horizon leaves out not only the "barbarian" countries north of the Danube and the German colonies of Cologne and Trier, but also such Roman provinces as Cisalpine Gaul with its important capital, Mediolanum (Milan), and Transalpine Gaul with an equally prominent capital, Lugdunum (Lyons), not to speak of Narbo Martius (Narbonne), Nemausus (Nîmes), and many other commercial and administrative centers, active hubs of Roman presence since the days of Caesar and Augustus. Even the communities in which he exercises his activity are only small and even diminutive congregations. Thus, in the case of Corinth, Murphy-O'Connor presumes that it counted only some forty members.[17] This may be too low an estimate. It is difficult to see how so limited a group could have accumulated all the problems and divisions that were addressed in the two letters sent to them. At any rate, the Christian presence was minimal amid a population of some one hundred thousand inhabitants.[18] There is no reason to suppose that the situation was different at Thessalonica, Philippi, or Ephesus.

---

17. J. Murphy-O'Connor, *Paul: A Critical Life* (Oxford: Clarendon, 1996), 278.

18. It is difficult to give an accurate estimate of the population of Corinth. Estimates vary from seventy thousand to seven hundred thousand. Cf. J. Murphy-O'Connor, "Corinth," *NIDB,* 1:734.

The resulting image of the Christian presence in the Roman Empire is that of tiny groups lost in cities that had begun turning into human anthills. By comparison, we may think of the Christian presence presently in the great Asian megalapolises, from Mumbai and Delhi to Shanghai and Tokyo.

These observations are not meant to belittle the missionary zeal of Paul. What he accomplished, or rather "what Christ accomplished through" him (Rom. 15:18), baffles human capacities. Yet, like any human achievement, the Apostle's labors cannot but have limitations. However, in the conclusion of this letter to the Romans, casting a global look at his ministry, he declares: "I have fulfilled the ministry of the Gospel of Christ" (Rom. 1:19). How are we to understand this statement?[19]

Obviously, Paul does not gauge his ministry in terms of quantitative and statistical data. Unlike Luke, who is interested in numbers (Acts 1:12; 2:41; 4:4; cf. 1:47; 5:14; 6:1–7; 9:31; 11:21; 16:5), Paul does not give an estimate of his results. He does not boast of having converted the Roman Empire or of having transformed the whole world into Christendom. "He thought in representative terms . . . without counting noses."[20] What matters is the significance of these small *ekklēsiai*. As he says of a new Christian, "first fruit for Christ in Asia" (Rom. 16:5; cf. 1 Cor. 16:15), he intends to present to Christ the "first fruits" of the eschatologi-

---

19. The translation and meaning of this text are discussed. Is the word *euangelion* to be understood in the passive sense ("the contents of the Gospel") or in the active sense ("the proclamation of the Gospel"). The active sense is taken by most of the English versions (ESV, NAB, NJB, NIB, NRSV). Note the bold "dynamic" rendering of Tyndale: "I have filled all countries with the Good Tydyings of Christ" versus Douay version: "I have replenished the Gospel." For Paul, the Good Tidings of the Resurrection of Christ constitute the accomplishment to which nothing can be added. Moreover, the verb *plēroō* used in the perfect refers to an accomplished plenitude and not to a progressive one.

20. E. O. Sanders, *Paul the Law and the Jewish People* (Philadelphia: Fortress Press, 1983), 189. "This representative missionary method focused on the great centers" (D. Zeller, *Der Brief an die Römer* [RNT; Regensburg: Pustet, 1984], 242).

cal harvest. It is only the first fruits, but they have the value of first fruits, partaking of the power of the Risen Lord, promise of the final victory of life over death (1 Cor. 15:20–25). The harvest belongs to God (1 Cor. 3:5–9).[21] In other words, Paul has made the voice of the gospel to resound in sufficiently representative places. From there it will echo all over the world. In this way, Paul can apply to the present days the words of Psalm 19:5: "Their voice has gone out to all the earth, and their words to the ends of the world" (Rom. 10:18).

Grafted on the stem of Israel, the nations share in the condition of Israel as a "small remnant." Following upon the disasters that befell the people of Israel, the prophets had expressed their faith in the divine intervention in favor of the "remnant" (Mic. 5:6; Zeph. 3:12; Isa. 4:4; 10:22; 28:5; Jer. 23:3; 31:7, etc.). This remnant evoked the tragedies of Israel's history. But it brought also to mind God's faithfulness to the Alliance. The remnant was not a lifeless stump to be thrown away. It is a living stock, a "holy seed" (Isa. 6:13). The incoming of the nations shows that vitality. Like the remnant of Israel, the *ekklēsiai* are small. Like the plenitude of Israel, the plenitude of the nations belongs to God when, at the end of times, all things will be put in his subjection and he will be "all in all" (1 Cor. 15:28). Presently, small as they may be, these *ekklēsiai*, as communities of faith and love, anticipate and embody already the eschatological plenitude "shining as lights in the world" (Phil. 2:15), "irradiating the knowledge of the glory of God shining on the face of Christ" (2 Cor. 4:6).

The Small Remnant Today

Paul's project is not based on statistics. It is eschatological and representative. It is eschatological in the sense that the gatherings of all the peoples in the loving embrace of the Father can only be an act of God and belongs to the end of times. This does not mean that we have only to wait passively

---

21. Cf. G. Biguzzi, "Paolo e la strategia apostolica della primizia," *Euntes Docete* 62 (2009): 75–100.

till the times are accomplished. "The time is fulfilled." "Behold now is the favorable time; now is the day of salvation" (2 Cor. 6:2). The mission of the Apostle is to enact the advent of the day, to realize the "first fruits" of the gathering of the people through communities responding by faith to the dynamics of the divine love revealed by Jesus on the cross.

This perspective is a challenge to the "old churches" as well as to the "young churches." The "old churches" are called to a New Evangelization. The "young churches" find themselves in a minority situation, often minimal in the midst of the human masses of Asia and Africa. What are, for instance, the .03 per-cent of Christians in Japan or Thailand, the 2.5 percent in India, Pakistan, or Bangladesh? Should we then speak of the failure of the mission? Or rather thank the Lord of the harvest for the sheaves already gathered and revive the dynamism of the advent of the Kingdom? Similarly, for the "old churches." Should we lament the empty churches, the shrinking religious practice, the paganization of society and moral standards? Or rather, following the example of Paul, should we face afresh the challenge to turn the "old churches" into young *ekklēsiai*, com-munities irradiating faith, hope, and charity, "shining like lights in the world" (Phil. 2:15), spreading "the knowledge of the glory of God in the face of Jesus Christ" (2 Cor. 4:6)? The call of the Apostle challenges equally "young" and "old" churches: "the hour has come for you to wake from sleep. For salvation is nearer to us now than when we first believed. The night is far gone; the day is at hand. So then let us cast off the works of darkness and put on the armor of light" (Rom. 13:11–12).

Conclusion

In the Acts of the Apostles, Luke depicts, with a touch of humor, the amused way the Athenians looked at "this preacher of for-eign deities" (Acts 17:18). For the Areopagus intelligentsia, Paul looked like one more of those itinerant philosophers who went from town to town peddling their speculations. For the Roman administration, he would have been rather one of those excited

Jews produced by the Diaspora. As for the Jews of the Diaspora, they might at first have welcomed a co-religionist, but they were soon shocked and outraged by his radical language. Finally, they were all disconcerted because neither the style nor the contents of his message fitted with the typology of the rhetors, rabbis, or agitators commonly found in the Mediterranean world.

Actually, the Pauline project is specific. It is essentially Jewish and communitarian.[22] It is rooted in the election of Israel but characterized by a new conception of Israelite identity. The Resurrection of the Messiah means that now have come the times of the new covenant according to the Spirit (1 Cor. 11:25; 2 Cor. 3:6). The People of God are now called to extend to its universal dimensions and to open itself to the "plenitude of the nations" (Rom. 11:25). Then will "Israel be saved" (Rom. 11:26). All along the Apostle of the Nations has his people Israel in mind and carries them in his heart, even and mostly when he invites them to get free from the Law and to integrate "the circumcised of heart."

The Pauline strategy does not stop with individual conversions. The target is the formation of a people. This is expressed particularly by the term *ekklēsia*, which brings to mind the gathering of the people of Israel to receive and commemorate the covenant at the foot of Mount Sinai or in the temple of Jerusalem. Gathering the Israel of the new covenant according to the Spirit: such is the divine project of which Paul is called to be the servant. It will be the guideline of his mission.

The situation will change for the following generation after the death of Paul. Pastoral letters respond to new needs. The Apostle has disappeared; his successors have now to secure the stability and the continuity of his project and to set up a leadership that will relay the apostolic authority. The dynamic conception of the *ekklēsia* will give way to a more sedate form of structure. Anyway the word *ekklēsia* appears rarely (1 Tim. 3:5,

---

22. It is the point on which I differ from L. J. Lietaert Perbolte, *Paul the Missionary* (CBET 34; Leuven: Peeters, 2003), which lays the stress on the proclamation of the gospel.

15; 5:16) and only in 3:15 will it have a theological connotation: "you will know how one ought to behave in the household of God, which is the church of the living God, a pillar and buttress of the truth" (1 Tim. 3:15). As noted by Gourgues, the image is no longer that of a house being built, as in 1 Corinthians 3:10–15, but of a "completed building within which the service of faith can be conducted (3:15a). A picture of 'domestication' will then apply . . . as against that of a liberty of development, of movement on the way, of exploration and of newness."[23] The same applies to the qualities required in the *episkopos* in 1 Timothy 3:1–7. They evoke "pastoral stability" rather than "missionary mobility."[24]

The New Testament canon has fittingly connected these two aspects of the Pauline inheritance. On the one hand, "pastoral stability" had to be secured by instituting a leadership that would succeed the authority of the departed founder and give guidance to the flock in the midst of a profusion of charisms and of doctrines. This was done by the Pastoral Epistles. On the other hand, the flame of the Spirit had to be kept alive. Written at the same time as the Pastoral Epistles, the Acts of the Apostles gives the image of "missionary mobility." By situating the Pauline ministry in the framework of the journey, Acts made Paul into a kind of apostolic Ulysses, the emblematic figure of the itinerant mission summarized in the program of Acts 1:7: "from Jerusalem to the ends of the earth." At the same time, Luke kept to the Pauline idea of a universalism rooted in Israel. It is the beautiful prospect outlined in the canticle of Simeon in Luke 2:32: "a light for revelation to the Gentiles and for glory to your people Israel." Paul would have recognized his project in these words.

---

23. M. Gourgues, *Les deux lettres à Timothée: La lettre à Tite* (CBNT 14; Paris: Cerf, 2009), 120–21. It will be noted that Gourgues proposes another version of 3:15. "Comment il faut se comporter dans la maison de Dieu qui est l'Église du Dieu vivant: en colonne et socle de la vérité." It is Timothy who is to be "colonne et socle."

24. Gourgues, *Les deux lettres*, 120.

7

The Project of Paul: Belonging to the Ekklēsia

Since Paul does not write theology or pastoral treatises but letters, he does not present what could be called an "ecclesiology." Neither does he propose a systematic description of what an ideal *ekklēsia* should be. For instance, he does not seem to be much concerned about structures. He accepts the ways communities organize themselves, even though he may have occasionally to set them right. At Thessalonica, there are "leaders" in the plural (1 Thess. 5:12). In Corinth, the list of the gifts of Spirit mentions gifts of leadership, but they take the penultimate place, far behind the apostles, prophets, and teachers (1 Cor. 12:28). Having *episkopoi* and *diakonoi* (Phil. 1:1), the church at Philippi anticipates a terminology that will eventually be canonized. For Paul, structures were of secondary importance since the true authority was that of the Apostle himself, father and founder, an authority that he had received directly from Christ (Gal. 1:11–12). His concern, his "anxiety for all the churches" (2 Cor. 11:28), was that the new communities of believers should be genuine communities of the new covenant according to the Spirit. It would be out of point here to draw a detailed description of what the Pauline communities were and what they were expected to be.[1]

---

1. Cf H. Hauser, *L'église à l'âge apostolique* (LD 164; Paris: Cerf, 1996), 67–106; V. Fusco, *Les premières communautés chrétiennes* (LD 188; Paris: Cerf, 2001), 223–334.

We may only consider a few salient interventions of the Apostle that reveal what he considered to be a genuine *ekklēsia* and what he expected the churches of the nations to be.

The efforts of the Apostle will consistently aim at bringing the communities to the essentials, to life in Christ. Such will be the case for the rites of belonging to the ecclesial community, Baptism and Lord's Supper. So will it be also, in the context of the charismatic excesses, when he will recall "the more excellent way" of faith, hope, and charity, which constitute the soul of belonging to Christ and to the People of God (1 Cor. 13:13).

At the Heart of the Rites of Belonging

Belonging to the community of the new covenant will necessarily be manifested in external ways through rites and expressions of shared common identity. In prayer meetings, participants sing together, listen to a teaching coming from the apostles, or to a message uttered by a prophet. Occasionally they will speak in tongues, but Paul cautions them against what could turn into wild cacophony (1 Cor. 14:6–11). The priority must remain with the "building up of the church" (1 Cor. 14:12, 17). Christian authenticity is defined by what is in the heart of the *ekklēsia*, "faith at work in love" (Gal. 5:6; cf. 1 Cor. 13).

Baptism

According to Acts, which reports a number of conversions, Baptism in the name of Jesus is a step expressing conversion and constitutes the initiation rite to enter the community of believers (Acts 2:42; 8:16, 36–38; 10:47–48; 16:15, 33; 18:8; 19:3–5). Since Paul addresses his letters to Christians who have already been baptized, he does not mention this role of Baptism. Taken out of context, one of his statements might even be misunderstood as a disparagement of Baptism: "Christ did not send me to baptize but to proclaim the gospel" (1 Cor. 1:17). Actually, the context shows that he wanted to caution the faithful against an undue attachment to the person of the baptizer, as philosophers identified themselves in terms of the master they followed as Platonists,

Pythagoreans, Epicureans, Aristotelians, etc. He opposes the distortion that would reduce Baptism to a rite of clannish initiation. The *ekklēsia* is not coterie but communion. In this context he can happily recall having given a few baptisms (1 Cor. 1:14–16). Others also, like Apollos, had baptized the Corinthian Christians. As for Paul, he lays the stress on his essential vocation to be the eschatological messenger of the new times. As Allo and Conzelmann say in their commentaries, anybody can baptize, but to Paul especially it has been given to meet the Risen Lord and to carry to the nations the Good News of the Resurrection.

Paul does not spurn Baptism. He refers to it several times. He recalls the baptismal confession of faith (Rom. 10:9–10; 1 Cor. 12:3). He invites the community to perceive its deep significance: "you were washed, you were sanctified, you were justified in the name of the Lord Jesus Christ and by the Spirit of our God" (1 Cor. 6:11). Baptism gives access to a community, but this community consists in belonging to the same body, the body of Christ, animated by the same Spirit: "For in one Spirit we were all baptized into one body, Jews or Greeks, slaves or free, and all were made to drink of one Spirit" (1 Cor. 12:13). The baptismal immersion is immersion and integration in the paschal mystery:

> Do you not know that all of us who have been baptized into Christ Jesus were baptized into his death? We were buried therefore with him by baptism into death, in order that, just as Christ was raised from the dead by the glory of the Father, we too might walk in newness of life. For if we have been united with him in a death like his, we shall certainly be united with him in a Resurrection like his. We know that our old self was crucified with him in order that the body of sin might be brought to nothing, so that we would no longer be enslaved to sin. For one who has died has been set free from sin. Now if we have died with Christ, we believe that we will also live with him. (Rom. 6:3–8)

Baptism was understood as a gesture of conversion and a rite of admission in the ecclesial community. Paul explains that the admission in the community is integration in the body of Christ and that conversion means participation in his death and Resurrection. He invites the community to go beyond the ritual aspect to enter the mystery of the new life in the Spirit.

The Lord's Supper

Reference to the Lord's Supper is less frequent in the letters of Paul. However, the way in which he speaks of it shows its importance in the life of the communities. In Mediterranean culture, meals were a privileged place of convivial gatherings. Brotherhoods and other *collegia* as well as the adepts of mystery cults gathered round a table. Even philosophers recalled the "banquet" of Socrates and tried to imitate it. The Jewish Passover, feast of the liberation of Israel, consisted essentially in a family ceremonial meal in which the Paschal Lamb was the main dish accompanied with several cups of wine. They "ate the Passover" (Mark 14:12, 14), "feasted the Passover" (1 Cor. 5:8). This was the setting in which Jesus celebrated the Last Supper with his disciples.

The Corinthian community celebrated the Lord's Supper in this sociocultural setting. But it was an ambiguous setting. The gatherings of Hellenistic *thiasoi* and other religious brotherhoods tended to be rather noisy and even bacchic. The banquets of the Roman *collegia* strengthened the solidarity of the association but also developed a spirit of clan and caste. This is what happened in Corinth: "in eating, each one goes ahead with his own meal. One goes hungry, another gets drunk" (1 Cor. 11:21). Murphy-O'Connor depicts the situation in the context of the great Roman *domus* in which a rich Christian, possibly the Gaius mentioned in 1 Corinthians 1:14 and Romans 16:23, hosted the community.[2] Inside, the dining room or *triclinium*, a pleasant space,

---

2. J. Murphy-O'Connor, *Keys to First Corinthians, Revisiting the Major Issues* (Oxford: Oxford University Press, 2003), 182–93; cf. G. Theissen, "Social Integration and Sacramental Activity. An Analysis of 1 Cor 11,17–34," in *Essays on Corinth: The Social Setting of Pauline Christianity* (ed. J. H. Schütz; Edinburgh: T. & T. Clark, 1983), 145–74; L. Legrand, "The First Eucharistic Heresy: 1 Cor 11:17–34," in *The Man's Harvest: Festschrift in Honor of Prof. B. Joseph Francis* (ed. S. Pinto and A.

lined with couches, is reserved for the close friends of the host. Stretched comfortably, they get first choice dishes and wines. The others, undistinguished common folk people, have to squeeze in the entrance courtyard, the *atrium*, where they receive meager fare and cheap wine.[3] Paul does not specify at which moment the Lord's Supper was commemorated. It might have been at the end of the meal, as a thanksgiving. Paul does not hesitate to state that some of the guests were drunk. He is indignant:

> I do not commend you, because when you come together it is not for the better but for the worse. For, in the first place, when you come together as a church, I hear that there are divisions among you. . . . When you come together, it is not the Lord's Supper that you eat. For in eating, each one goes ahead with his own meal. One goes hungry, another gets drunk. What! Do you not have houses to eat and drink in? Or do you despise the church of God and humiliate those who have nothing? (1 Cor. 11:18–22)

It is interesting to note that the first eucharistic heresy to be condemned did not refer to orthodoxy but to orthopraxy. Neglecting the poor amounts to despising the church of God.

Lawrence; Bangalore: ATC, 2016), 85–98; M. Quesnel, *La première épître aux Corinthiens* (CBNT 7; Paris: Cerf, 2018), 271–73.

3. A letter of Pliny illustrates this practice. "I came to be dining with a man who thought he combined elegance with economy, but who appeared to me to be both mean and lavish, for he set the best dishes before himself and a few others and treated the rest to cheap and scrappy food. He had apportioned the wine in small decanters of three different kinds, not in order to give his guests their choice but so that they might not refuse. He had one kind for himself and us, another for his less distinguished friends— for he is a man who classifies his acquaintances—and a third for his own freedmen and those of his guests. The man who sat next to me noticed this and asked me if I approved of it. I said no. 'Then how do you arrange matters?' he asked. 'I set the same before all,' I answered, 'for I invite my friends to dine not to grade them one above the other, and those whom I have set at equal places at my board and on my couches I treat as equals in every respect.' 'What! even the freedmen?' he said. 'Yes,' I replied, 'for then I regard them as my guests at table, not as freedmen'" (Pliny, *Letters* 2.6).

When the divisions and exclusions of Roman society entered the Christian assembly, the very nature of the *ekklēsia* was undermined and the basic communion of the "sons of God in Jesus Christ" was ruined. As Paul says elsewhere, "For as many of you as were baptized into Christ have put on Christ. There is neither Jew nor Greek, there is neither slave nor free, there is no male and female, for you are all one in Christ Jesus" (Gal. 3:27–28).

For upper-class Corinthians, the celebration of the Lord's Supper was an occasion to meet and cheer together. Paul has to remind them of the grave and even tragic nature of this celebration as it commemorates what took place "on the night when he was betrayed":

> For I received from the Lord what I also delivered to you, that the Lord Jesus on the night when he was betrayed took bread, and when he had given thanks, he broke it, and said, "This is my body which is for you. Do this in remembrance of me." In the same way also he took the cup, after supper, saying, "This cup is the new covenant in my blood. Do this, as often as you drink it, in remembrance of me." For as often as you eat this bread and drink the cup, you proclaim the Lord's death until he comes. Whoever, therefore, eats the bread or drinks the cup of the Lord in an unworthy manner will be guilty concerning the body and blood of the Lord. Let a person examine himself, then, and so eat of the bread and drink of the cup. (1 Cor. 11:23–28)

The commemoration of the Last Supper is that of a body "handed over" and of a "blood shed for the multitude." Participating in it means "participating in the blood and body of Christ" (1 Cor. 10:16). "Let a person examine himself, then, and so eat of the bread and drink of the cup" and fully realize the significance of the act accomplished. Unworthy participation is a sin against "the body and blood of the Lord."

Do this in remembrance of me" (11:25). In the biblical sense of the term, commemoration, or *anamnesis* in liturgical language, does not consist only in bringing back to mind an event lost in the past. It actualizes it, re-presents it in the full sense of the term. At the first Passover, at the time of the Exodus, the Lord had said: "This day shall be for you a day of commemoration, and you shall keep it as a feast to the Lord; throughout your generations, as a statute forever, you shall keep it as a feast" (Exod. 12:14). The Sinai covenant had confirmed the election of Israel, and Deuteronomy specified: "The Lord our God made a covenant with us in Horeb. Not with our fathers did the Lord make this covenant, but with us, who are all of us here alive today" (Deut. 5:2–3). The Mishna commented: "At each generation, all should consider themselves as if they had personally come out of Egypt as the Scripture says: On that day, you will report it to your son in this way: 'This is what the Lord has done for me when I came out of Egypt.'"[4] At each generation, and for everyone, the commemoration made the salvific event a present reality.

This is what Paul means when referring to the commemoration of the body and blood of the new Passover. Commemorating means going to the heart of the paschal mystery. But why does he mention only the death of Christ? For him death and Resurrection are indissociable, as we saw, for instance, when he spoke of Baptism. But the Risen One is not a hazy ghostly appearance. He remains the one who was handed over for us to death on a cross (Gal. 2:20; Rom. 5:8; 8:32). In a context where Corinthians took lightly the Lord's Supper, Paul emphasizes the tragic character of the paschal event. Moreover, he does not say "the death of Jesus" but "the death of the Lord." By saying "the Lord," he evokes the lordship of the one who will triumph over "every rule and every authority and power" and "deliver the Kingdom to God the Father . . . for he must reign until he has put all his enemies under his feet" (1 Cor. 15:24–25). In the phrase "the death of the Lord," the two words "death" and "Lord" form an antithesis that summarizes the paradoxical contrast between the kenosis

---

4. *Pesaḥ* 10.5. This *mishna* borrows the terms of the *hagaddah shel Pesaḥ*, the great paschal narrative which was an essential part of the paschal ritual.

of the Passion and the lordship of the Resurrection. This is what the Eucharist "commemorates" and re-presents by recalling the death of Jesus and anticipating his victory over death and the powers of evil.

"As often as you eat this bread and drink the cup, you proclaim the Lord's death until he comes" (11:25–26). Some commentators have suggested that the "proclamation" of the Lord's death referred to a homily that went along with the anamnesis[5] or to a reading of the Passion that would have preceded it.[6] Paul's thought goes deeper. The plural "you proclaim" does not refer to a preacher or a reader but to the entire community: what the community does is, by itself, "proclaiming." In the commemoration, the paschal event reaches the participants and resounds through them. As a commentator puts it, "the Eucharist is an acted sermon, an acted proclamation of the death which it commemorates."[7]

To conclude, it is noteworthy that Paul, "with the verb 'proclaim' (*katangellein*), uses a technical term of missionary language (e.g. 2:1; 9:14 in our epistle)."[8] "The language of mission loves such expressions as 'announce Christ' (Phil. 1:17; Col. 1:28) or 'Christ is announced' (Phil. 1:18). We have also phrases like 'announce the Good News' (1 Cor. 9:14), 'announce the Word of God' (Acts 13:5; 17:23), 'announce the Lord' (Acts 15:36)."[9] The eucharistic commemoration is at the root of mission activity. It provides the primordial link between the paschal event and its

---

5. Cf. J. Jeremias, *The Eucharistic Words of Jesus* (London: SCM, 1966), 106–7; H. Conzelmann, *Der erste Brief an die Corinther* (KEK 5; Göttingen: Vandenhoeck & Ruprecht, 1969), 238.

6. C. K. Barrett, *The First Epistle to the Corinthians* (HNTC; New York: Harper & Row, 1968), 270.

7. A. Robertson and A. Plummer, *A Critical and Exegetical Commentary on the First Epistle of St. Paul to the Corinthians* (ICC; Edinburgh: T. & T. Clark, 1999 [reprint]), 249.

8. D. Zieler, *Der erste Brief an die Corinther* (KEK 5; Göttingen: Vandenhoeck & Ruprecht 2009), 238.

9. J. Schniewind, art. *angellō, TDNT* 1.71–72, which notes the use of the verb *katangellein*.

proclamation by the church. The commemoration of the body handed over and of the shed blood is the seminal missionary action that will unfold in the evangelizing proclamation to the nations.

At the Heart of the Gifts of the Spirit

In the world of the nations, Christian communities coexisted with the *collegia* and *thiasoi* of the Greco-Roman world or the philosophical sects and the oriental cults that flourished in the Mediterranean countries. Corinthian Christians were tempted to imitate their practices, and even their eccentricities. In meetings that turned hurly-burly Paul feels obliged to recall what is essential, "faith, hope, and love" (1 Cor. 13:13). In the first letter that he wrote, in the beginning and in the conclusion of his message to one of the first churches of the nations, he identifies the fundamental triptych as the distinctive sign of Christian authenticity. "We give thanks to God always . . . remembering before our God and Father your work of faith and labor of love and steadfastness of hope in our Lord Jesus Christ" (1 Thess. 1:3; cf. 5:8). It would exceed the limits of this study to develop *in extenso* these basic themes of Pauline theology. We can only situate them in the context of his apostolic mission.

Faith

Faith is one of the main themes of Pauline theology. The noun (*pistis*) occurs 91 times in the authentic letters and the verb (*pisteuein*), 44 times. Among the many texts dealing with faith, we may single out Romans 10:14–17, which presents faith as the final outcome of the evangelizing process.

> "Everyone who calls on the name of the Lord will be saved." How then will they call on him in whom they have not believed? And how are they to believe in him of whom they have never heard? And how are they to hear without someone preaching? And how are they to preach unless they are sent? As it is written, "How beautiful are the feet of those

who preach the good news!" But they have not all obeyed the gospel. For Isaiah says, "Lord, who has believed what he has heard from us?" So, faith comes from hearing, and hearing through the word of Christ. (Rom. 10:13–17)

These verses are part of Paul's reflection on the failure of the proclamation of the message to Israel (Rom. 9–11). The offer of salvation has been universal. The Good News has been heard everywhere. The words of Psalm 19:5 can be applied to the proclamation of the gospel. "Their voice has gone out to all the earth, and their words to the ends of the world" (Rom. 10:18). Paul may think of the considerable stir that the news of the messianic Resurrection should have raised in the Diaspora. Yet that voice has not been heard. It was a disappointing response from the people of Israel and, on the contrary, an unexpected welcome from the pagans. Taking note of this situation, Paul considers the mysterious process leading from the sending of the messenger to faith that "invokes the Lord." He does it by analyzing the chain going from invocation to faith, from faith to hearing, from hearing to proclamation, and finally to sending. We seem to go through the headings of the successive chapters of a mission theology.

The previous chapters have already considered the first stages. First was the *mission*, the sending of the missionary, commissioned to announce the Good News: mission is *missio Dei*. Then comes the *proclamation*, which is not arguing about a thesis but the announcement of an event, the paschal event. The object of the proclamation is *"the word of Christ"* (v. 17). This can be understood as a word coming from Christ, of which Christ is the author, or as a word about Christ, of which Christ is the object. In the sense of a "word coming from Christ," the stress bears on the authority of the Lord who is its guarantor. In the sense of "word about Christ," it evokes the entire contents of the Good News concerning Christ, the Risen Lord, the sum total of the entire apostolic message (1 Cor. 15:12), the crucified Messiah, wisdom and power of God (1 Cor. 1:23), ultimately the Son of God (2 Cor. 1:19).

The response to the "word of Christ" is *hearing*. "How to

believe without first hearing?" "Hearing" is the first step of the return to God. The invisible God does not connect with humanity through visions but through his word." "In the beginning was the Word" (John 1:1). *Shema Israel*: "Hear, Israel": it is the basic attitude that the God of the covenant requires from his people (Deut. 6:4). The *Shema* will be the prayer in which Israel finds its identity. It is resumed by Jesus (Mark 12:29). It is a hearing that opens the heart to the message. It is an attentive hearing. One can hear without paying attention, as in the case of those who heard and have rejected the Good News, as announced by Isaiah (vv. 18–21 quoting Isa. 65:2). Faith consists in heeding and assimilating the "language of the Cross" (1 Cor. 1:18).

It is an *interior hearing*, a hearing of the heart. As the previous verses have it: "The word is near you, in your mouth and in your heart (that is, the word of faith that we proclaim); because, if you confess with your mouth that Jesus is Lord and believe in your heart that God raised him from the dead, you will be saved" (Rom. 10:8–9). The believer to whom is given this listening of the heart joins Paul on the Damascus way who received "in" him the revelation of the Son of God (Gal. 1:16). Faith consists in identifying with the experience of the encounter with the Risen One, in discovering "the power of the Resurrection," in letting "shine in our hearts the light of the knowledge of the glory of God in the face of Jesus Christ" (2 Cor. 4:6).

It is a *hearing in obedience*. It consists in "obeying the Good News." What this hearing signifies appears in the link that connects in Greek the words "hearing" (*akoē*) and "obedience" (*hyp-akoē*), "submitting" (*hypo*) to what is heard. This "hearing" is that of the ear that leans humbly to receive the impulse of the word, grasp it, and absorb it fully. Faith is obedient listening, as the phrase has it: "obedience of faith" (Rom. 1:5; 16:26).

But obedience does not mean passivity. At the time of the Exodus, to the divine word coming from Mount Sinai, the people have responded by the commitment of the covenant: "All that the Lord has spoken we will do and we will be obedient" (Exod. 24:7). It is so also in the new covenant. Faith is commitment with the difference that the commitment does not consist in the "works of the Law" but in letting oneself be permeated by the grace of God, be transfigured by it, and be infused by the love of Christ. Faith leads to love: it is "faith working through love" (Gal. 5:6). Faith and charity are indissociably associated (1 Thess. 1:3; 3:6; 5:8; Phlm. 5). By opening itself to the divine design, faith assumes the dimensions of the divine purpose, enters "the depth of the riches and wisdom and knowledge of God" (Rom. 11:33), and partakes of its dynamism.

In short, for Paul, faith, the distinctive mark of the members of the *ekklēsia*, consists in being open to the Spirit, "who searches everything, even the depths of God, . . . the Spirit who is from God, that we might understand the things freely given us by God" (1 Cor. 2:10–12). Through faith, the believer's mind and life are moved by the Spirit; he opens himself to "God's love poured into our hearts through the Holy Spirit who has been given to us" (Rom. 5:5).

Love

At this juncture, we come again across a problem of language. The Greek word for "love" is *agapē*. It occurs frequently in the Pauline writings.[10] It is less frequent in Greek literature, which prefers *erōs* (love as desire, not only "erotic" but also esthetic), and *philia* (disinterested, "philanthropic" love). In the Septuagint, the Greek translators of the Bible had already opted for the rare term *agapē* to qualify a love responding to the covenant. The English translation poses a problem. Common use has stretched the use of the term to apply it from the gustative ("I love mangoes") to the erotic field ("to make love"). As for the word "char-

---

10. In Paul, the noun *agapē* occurs 75 times and the verb *agapan* 33 times. Adding the adjective *agapētos* (beloved, 27 times), we come to a total of 135 references to "love" in the Pauline corpus. A similar frequency can be found only in the Johannine works. In John's gospel the noun occurs 7 times and the verb 36 times; in John's epistles, the noun *agapē* is used 21 times, the verb *agapan* 31 times and the adjective *agapētos* 10 times. In the entire New Testament, the frequency of the noun is 116, of the verb 141, and of the adjective 61.

ity," it is often understood as synonymous with "alms." However, we shall retain these two words, leaving it to the context to specify their precise biblical meaning. We shall keep in mind that, in Paul's writings, speaking of "charity" refers to a move from the heart while "love" has the depth of the "abiding Spirit."

What "love" means has been manifested in the gift God made of his Son "handed over for us" (Rom. 8:32).

> For while we were still weak, at the right time Christ died for the ungodly. For one will scarcely die for a righteous person—though perhaps for a good person one would dare even to die—but God shows his love for us in that while we were still sinners, Christ died for us. (Rom. 5:6–8)

The text describes unconditional, sacrificial love, even unto death. It is a love beyond human capacity, proper to God. However, God gives human beings to partake of it since "God's love has been poured into our hearts through the Holy Spirit who has been given to us" (Rom. 5:5). In the context, it is clear that "God's love" is not the love that we could have for God but the love that God gives us, and which is God's own nature. As 1 John 4:10 puts it, "In this is love, not that we have loved God but that he loved us and sent his Son to be the propitiation for our sins" (1 John 4:10). The Spirit of God who "alone knows what is in God" (1 Cor. 2:11) "knows" the "God of love" (2 Cor. 11:11, 13) and imparts this divine power of love. It is this love that makes us "children of God, led by the Spirit of God" (Rom. 8:14). It becomes the distinctive mark of the believer. By the Spirit, the believer lives in communion with the divine love manifested in the sacrificial gift of the Son. It finds renewed strength in this communion with that radical surrender revealed by the "face of Christ."

The Apostle finds strength in the power of this love. He sings it in the triumphal Ode to Victorious Love in Romans 8:31–39. It is the conclusion of the first part of the letter. It described the new life in the Spirit received through faith. This long exposition concludes with a prayer of passionate admiration at the gift of God. "He who did not spare his own Son but gave him up for us all, how will he not also with him graciously give us all things?" (Rom. 8:32).

Who shall separate us from the love of Christ? Shall tribulation, or distress, or persecution, or famine, or nakedness, or danger, or sword? As it is written, "For your sake we are being killed all the day long; we are regarded as sheep to be slaughtered." No, in all these things we are more than conquerors through him who loved us. For I am sure that neither death nor life, nor angels nor rulers, nor things present nor things to come, nor powers nor height nor depth, nor anything else in all creation, will be able to separate us from the love of God in Christ Jesus our Lord. (Rom. 8:34–39)

"The love of Christ" in the beginning of the passage and "the love of God in Christ Jesus" at the end frame the dangers, distress, and trials of apostolic life and transform it into victory. The Apostle does not view himself as a Stoic who would be able to face undisturbed all kinds of hardship. That would still be a display of pride, "glorifying in the flesh." It is an act of faith in the unutterable love manifested in God's surrender of his Son. Neither does he speak of the love that he would have for Christ and for God and that would enable him to face all trials out of love. The strength would still emanate from himself; it would be *his* love that would strengthen him. But it is not *his* strength and *his* love that uphold him. It is the love that God has manifested in Jesus Christ and handed over through the Spirit who infused a divine source of strength. It is "through him who loved us" that the Apostle is victorious. It is the divine love that is victorious. It has a power that exceeds infinitely the limits of any human strength that Paul sees at work in his life and that he sings in this vibrant hymn to the triumphal power of love.

The other ode to love is also well known.[11] But whereas, in Romans 8, Paul turned a contemplative look at Christ and divine love, in 1 Corinthians 13, he considers this love as it is at work

---

11. Cf. C. Spicq, *AGAPE in the New Testament: Analyse des textes* (EB; Paris: Gabalda, 1959), 2:53–120; B. Standaert, "1 Corinthiens 13," in *Charisma und Agape (1 Ko 12–14)* (ed. L. De Lorenzi; Rome: St. Paul's Abbey, 1983), 127–39.

in human life. The context deals with the problem of charisms. They grew so wildly that they had come to disturb the life of the community. Chapter 12 recalls that the variety of gifts must operate within the unity of the body of Christ. Chapter 14 applies this principle in practical instructions. Between these two chapters, chapter 13 seems at first to be a digression: from charisms we shift to *agapē*. But finally, the digression brings the matter to what is essential. Particular charisms are subordinate to the fundamental gifts: faith, hope, and charity. On account of the apparent digression and of the change of style, some commentators have concluded that chapter 13 is an extraneous element, possibly a hymn of the early church that Paul would have inserted in his exposition. But we can as well see the chapter as his own composition; he was a skilled author, able to use the interplay of a variety of literary forms. At any rate, whether the text comes directly from Paul's hand or he borrowed it and inserted it, this flight of poetry fits the context and responds well to the Corinthian situation.

Though the term of "hymn" is commonly used, the poem should be more fittingly entitled the Eulogy of Love.[12] The literary form of eulogy or *enkomion* was classical in antiquity. It consisted in singing the praises of a famous figure, alive or diseased, of a virtue, or, ironically, of a vice.[13]

A typical example is the Eulogy of Wisdom in Wisdom 7:22–8:1. The two eulogies show interesting similarities. Both begin describing the qualities attached to the virtues that they raise. But the Eulogy of Wisdom goes on setting forth the theological ground of these qualities. "She is a breath of the might of God and a pure emanation of the glory of the Almighty; therefore, nothing defiled can enter into her. For she is the reflection of eternal light, the spotless mirror of the power of God, the image

---

12. As M. Quesnel puts it, "the term of 'hymn' does not seem to be fitting since the features of a poetical composition are missing" (*La première épître aux Corinthiens* (CBNT 7; Paris: Cerf, 2018), 314.

13. Like the Eulogy of the Parasite of Lucian and, later on, the Eulogy of Folly of Erasmus.

of his goodness" (Wis. 7:25–26). But in the Eulogy of Love in 1 Corinthians 13, this theological aspect is missing. A surprising feature of the text is that neither God nor Christ nor the Spirit is mentioned. "The reader is under the impression of a shift from the theological to the anthropological level."[14] However, given the context and the Pauline background, we can hardly presume that the text represents an atheistic or secular charity. Rather, with B. Standaert, we shall perceive in these verses a diffused Christology and theology. There are sufficient indications to suggest that this contemplation of *agapē* rests on a Trinitarian implicit infrastructure.[15]

- The introduction classified love among the charisms. It is infinitely superior to them, but, like them, it is a gift of the *Spirit* (12:1–11). When we speak of the supreme charism of *agapē*, we imply the Spirit.
- The conclusion evokes the "face to face" encounter with God (v. 12), prefigured in the *agapē*. God is the focal point of life in *agapē*. God the Father and his love constitute the horizon of a life committed to love.
- The qualities of love listed in verses 4–7 echo the call to share in the kenotic humility of *Christ* in Philippians 2:2–5 and to "have in mind that which was in Christ Jesus." The texts of Philippians 2 and 1 Corinthians 13:4–7 dovetail perfectly. They describe the way to live "in Christ Jesus," who, "though he was in the form of God, did not count equality with God a thing to be grasped, but made himself nothing, taking the form of a servant, . . . and humbled himself by becoming obedient to the

---

14. J. Dupont, "Dimensions du problème des charismes dans 1 Cor 12–14," in *Charisma und Agape (1 Ko 12–14)*, 20–21.

15. B. Standaert, "1 Corinthiens 13," in *Charisma und Agape*, 132–34. "Ce qui peut étonner, c'est qu'à aucun moment le nom de Dieu ou celui du Christ ou encore l'Esprit Saint ne sont mentionnés. . . . Mais une lecture serrée laisse transparaître tant le nom du Christ que la présence du Christ ou celle de l'Esprit Saint" (B. Standaert, *Le ministère de Paul: Parole, prière, miséricorde* [Paris: Mediaspaul, 2016], 143).

point of death, even death on a cross" (Phil. 2:6–8). The song of love does not speak of Christ, but it cannot be understood apart from Christ.

We may conclude with B. Standaert:

> In his Eulogy of *agapē*, Paul reaches the essential thrust of life in Christ, as it is expressed in this passage of Phl 2:5-8. . . . What Paul calls *agapē* coincides with the deep level of Christian experience in which the human being is seized by grace, by justification and by the self-surrender of the crucified Christ. . . . We are finally brought to a transposition of the famous formula of the letter to the Galatians: "It is no longer I who live, but Christ who lives in me." (Gal. 2:20)[16]

Hope

Faith active in love is lived in a situation of tension between salvation "already" bestowed and "not yet" obtained. These two aspects of salvation experience are well expressed in a text of Romans 8:24–25.

Already.
> For all who are led by the Spirit of God are sons of God. For you did not receive the spirit of slavery to fall back into fear, but you have received the Spirit of adoption as sons, by whom we cry, "Abba! Father!" The Spirit himself bears witness with our spirit that we are children of God, and if children, then heirs, heirs of God and fellow heirs with Christ, provided we suffer with him in order that we may also be glorified with him. For I consider that the sufferings of this present time are not worth comparing with the glory that is to be revealed to us. (Rom. 8:14–18)

"Heirs of God and fellow heirs with Christ," "glorified with him": this means that, in love, the believer communes in the Love

---

16. Standaert, "1 Corinthiens 13," in *Charisma und Agape*, 132.

that God is, shares in "the power of the Resurrection of Christ," and with Christ, the first born, has already entered the "newness of life" (Rom. 6:4) and has become a "new creature" (2 Cor. 5:17; Gal. 6:15).

Not Yet. But Paul goes on to add:

> For the creation waits with eager longing for the revealing of the sons of God. For the creation was subjected to futility, . . . in hope that the creation itself will be set free from its bondage to corruption and obtain the freedom of the glory of the children of God. For we know that the whole creation has been groaning together in the pains of childbirth until now. And not only the creation, but we ourselves, who have the first fruits of the Spirit, groan inwardly as we wait eagerly for adoption as sons, the redemption of our bodies. For in this hope we were saved. Now hope that is seen is not hope. For who hopes for what he sees? But if we hope for what we do not see, we wait for it with patience. (Rom. 8:19–25)

Subjection to futility, bondage to corruption, pains of childbirth, groaning in expectation: Paul multiplies the images describing the fragility of the present human condition. Entering the new world of the Resurrection entails that "we suffer with him in order that we may also be glorified with him" in the certitude that "the sufferings of this present time are not worth comparing with the glory that is to be revealed to us." Glory and corruption coexist in the believer's life, but faith knows that the "glory" is more powerful than the "corruption," life than death, grace than sin (Rom. 5:20), the love of God in Jesus Christ than any power of death.

And Now? This hope will be translated in three attitudes: confidence, patience, and joy.

• *Confidence*: hope is "firm" (2 Cor. 1:7) since it rests on the divine promise that is irrevocable as it was for Abraham (Rom.

4:16). "Hope does not disappoint since the love of God has been poured in our heart by the Spirit given to us" (Rom. 5:5). Our hope has the strongest possible guarantee since it does not depend on human weakness and on the ups and downs of world events, but on the love that God has for us. It is an unconditional love as shown by Christ who "died for us while we were yet sinners" (Rom. 5:8). "What then shall we say to these things? If God is for us, who can be against us? He who did not spare his own Son but gave him up for us all, how will he not also with him graciously give us all things?" (Rom. 8:31–32).

- *Patience*: This certitude gives the courage of patience. Greek has two words for "patience." They express the two sides, active and passive, of the virtue of patience. One is *hypomonē*, literally the capacity "to hold on under" (trials, difficulties), endurance. It is a form of courage that the Apostle had to show, "afflicted in every way, but not crushed; perplexed, but not driven to despair; persecuted, but not forsaken; struck down, but not destroyed" (2 Cor. 4:8–9). The other word is *makrothymia*, literally "great character." It evokes the breadth of vision, the capacity to see the problems of present life in the perspectives of the divine plan and to open one's heart to the breath of the Spirit. This broad vision is primarily a divine attribute (Rom. 2:4; 9:22). It is a quality that Paul can claim (2 Cor. 6:6), one of the first fruits of the Spirit immediately after love, peace, and joy (Gal. 5:22).

- *Joy*: "joyful in hope, patient in tribulation" (Rom. 12:12). The courage of patience in tribulations is lived in joy. Jailed and facing possible death, Paul expresses his joy: "I rejoice. Yes, and I will rejoice" (Phil. 1:18). He invites the Philippians to share in this joy without lamenting his plight: "Even if I am to be poured out as a drink offering upon the sacrificial offering of your faith, I am glad and rejoice with you all. Likewise, you also should be glad and rejoice with me" (Phil. 2:17–18). Later on, an invitation to joy is the conclusion of his message.

Rejoice in the Lord always; again, I will say, Rejoice. Let your reasonableness be known to everyone. The Lord is

at hand; do not be anxious about anything, but in everything by prayer and supplication with thanksgiving let your
requests be made known to God. And the peace of God,
which surpasses all understanding, will guard your hearts
and your minds in Christ Jesus. (Phil. 4:4–7)

Joy is based on the hope in the return of the Lord. It is caused by
the sight of the fervor of the community, its "work of faith and
labor of love and steadfastness of hope in our Lord Jesus Christ"
(1 Thess. 1:3). It reflects the peace of God, which surpasses all
understanding (Phil. 4:7). In Galatians 5:22 also "charity, joy,
peace, patience" are linked together as the "first fruits of the
Spirit." When Thessalonians are disturbed by the first deaths in
the community, the Apostle invites them "not to grieve as others
who have no hope" (1 Thess. 4:13). Joy and peace based on hope
rooted in faith: such are the specific marks of the believer that
distinguish them from "others."

Paul would have had many reasons to give way to gloom and
discouragement. His missionary path was strewn with failures.
His hope had been that his Jewish people would welcome the
Good News massively and enthusiastically. Such was not the
case, and this remained a lingering anguish throughout his life.
To a certain extent, the conversion of the pagans made up for
this failure. But the communities that he founded fell short of
his expectations. The first letter to the Corinthians is a record of
whatever can go wrong amid poorly tutored new Christians. It
went from clannish divisions to doubts about the Resurrection,
going through a case of incest, adulterated eucharists, wavering
between sexual licentiousness and an Encratite condemnation of
marriage. In the following letter, the situation has further degen-
erated. The situation brought him to tears (2 Cor. 2:4). Corinthian
Christians have been seduced by smooth talkers who "peddle
the word of God" (2 Cor. 2:17). Galatians also have renounced
their allegiance to the Apostle and to his gospel as soon as he
turned his back. He responds to these disappointments by setting them in the dynamic of hope: "we rejoice in our sufferings,
knowing that suffering produces endurance, and endurance pro-

duces character, and character produces hope, and hope does not put us to shame, because God's love has been poured into our hearts through the Holy Spirit who has been given to us" (Rom. 5:3–5). Hope transcends the vicissitudes of the human condition by reaching the solid immovable ground of God's overpowering love poured in our hearts by the Spirit.

Conclusion

The mission project of the Apostle is communitarian. Its aim is to gather the People of God, transformed by the Spirit, in its eschatological universal plenitude. The churches that he founded among the nations are the first fruits of this plenitude in a representative manner. But communitarian perspective does not amount to soulless communal and clannish spirit. The People of the New Covenant are invited to join a "communion" that calls for the personal commitment of faith in Jesus Christ. It is a commitment to "live in Christ," to share in the "communion of the Son of God" (1 Cor. 1:9), communion to his body and blood (1 Cor. 10:16), "sharing in his sufferings to know the power of his Resurrection" (Phil. 3:10). A community united in "faith working through love": such is the divine project whose servant is Paul, and which governs his mission.

In his Damascus encounter with the Risen Lord, Paul received "the knowledge of the glory of God in the face of Jesus Christ." He turns the new Christians toward this face of Christ so that they too may share "in the illumination of the Gospel of the glory of God." It is this face of the Crucified and Risen Lord that he presents to those who have been baptized and who share in the Lord's Supper. It is this face that he exhorts the *ekklēsiai* of the nations to reflect in faith, hope, and charity so that they "may be blameless and innocent, children of God without blemish in the midst of a crooked and twisted generation, among whom [they] shine as lights in the world" (Phil. 2:15). Such was the project which the Apostle had in heart when he went about the teeming cities of the Mediterranean world.

8

The Mission Field

"Apostle to the Nations" (Rom. 11:13; Gal. 2:8–9; cf. Rom. 1:5; 15:16; 16:26): such is the title that Paul assumes and under which he continues to be known. It is a tribute to the zeal of one who took the gospel from Jerusalem to Rome and possibly to Spain. However, we need to cast a closer look at the extent of that mission field, not to belittle the zeal of the missionary but better to apprehend its scope.

"A Wide Door Is Opened to Me" (1 Corinthians 16:9)

Biblical atlases and Bible editions reproduce the map of Paul's journeys. Following the Acts of the Apostles, these maps retrace with precision three "missionary journeys," ending with a fourth "captivity journey." Commentators are more cautious. Particularly they question a distinction between a second and a third journey. The turning point between the two journeys is supposed to be in Acts 18:22 according to which, coming from Ephesus and landing at Caesarea, "he went up and greeted the church, and then went down to Antioch." It is usually presumed that "the church" was the "mother church" of Jerusalem. It may be so. But if Luke wanted to make this visit a turning point and a new start in the Pauline mission, he would have been more explicit. Hiding the Jerusalem visit behind a vague expression, the text suggests continuity rather than disruption. Did Luke intend to cut the impetus of the Word into slices? Did he exclude the "captivity journey" from this thrust? These are questions pertaining to the structure of the book of Acts.

The letters themselves raise another problem. They show Paul wayfaring to realize his project. But do they tally with the pattern of Acts? We know from the Gospel that Luke did not hesitate to modify the chronology of the events according to the needs of his theological purpose. An example is the visit of Jesus to Nazareth. Mark and Matthew place it in the middle of Jesus's ministry (Mark 6:1–6; Matt. 13:54–58) whereas Luke has it in the beginning, as a caption to the whole messianic program. On the sole basis of Paul's letters, attempts have been made to reconstitute the Pauline itineraries. For instance, according to Murphy-O'Connor, a single journey, starting from Antioch, would have taken the Apostle to Galatia, Macedonia, and Corinth between 45 and 50.[1] According to Galatians 4:13–15, the evangelization of Galatia would be due to the fortuitous incident of some health problem in the course of this single journey.

Anyway, the letters and Acts agree on a ministry that, starting from Antioch, covered Asia Minor, moved to Greece, Philippi, Thessalonica, Corinth, met with serious difficulties in Ephesus, and planned to reach Rome. The setting of the arrival in Rome differs in both sources. In the letter, the journey to Rome is a planned project. In Acts, it is the end of a long captivity. But both agree that the outcome is the proclamation of the Good News "with all boldness and without hindrance" (Acts 28:31), in the heart of the pagan world. Both describe a vast apostolic field that extends from western Asia to southern Europe.

---

1. J. Murphy-O'Connor, *Paul: A Critical Life* (New York: Oxford University Press, 1996), 24–28. This approach was initiated by G. Lüdemann, *Paulus der Heidenapostel: Studien zur Chronologie* (FRLANT 123; Göttingen: Vandenhoeck & Ruprecht, 1980; English translation, *Paul Apostle to the Gentiles* (London: SCM, 1984). A chronological table summarizes the hypothesis on pp. 272–73). See a comparative table of both chronologies in R. E. Brown, *Introduction to the New Testament* (New York: Doubleday, 1997), 428–29. See also Gregory Tatum, *New Chapters in the Life of Paul: The Relative Chronology of His Career* (CBQMS 41, Washington DC: Catholic Biblical Association of America, 2006), and book review in *ITS* 44 (2007): 311–21.

The geography of the letters is even more extensive than that of Acts since it extends to Arabia (Gal. 1:17), Damascus (Gal. 1:17; 2 Cor. 11:32), Illyricum (Rom. 15:19), and possibly even Spain (Rom. 15:24, 28). In that context, "Arabia" refers to Transjordan, from Damascus as far as the Nabatean kingdom and its capital Petra. It will be the first mission land of the Apostle.[2] The Roman province of Illyricum went from the Adriatic Sea to the Danube River, and so it covered the present-day countries of Albania, Croatia, and Hungary. Paul refers probably to the southern part of that area touching Macedonia. The Macedonian ministry would not have been restricted to the eastern part facing the Mediterranean Sea. It would have extended inland up to "Illyricum." As for Spain, it should be noted that the project was not outlandish. Since the victorious issue of the Punic wars, Hispania had become an integral part of the Roman Empire; it was even one of the provinces that had been most thoroughly Latinized. Great "Latin" authors such as Seneca, Quintilian, and Martial were from Spain. Regular sea-lines of communication brought to Rome such Spanish special goods as wheat, minerals (silver, copper, iron ore, tin, lead), and finished products (steel, linen). Gades (Cadix) had one of the most important shipyards of the Mediterranean world. With favorable wind, the sea journey from Ostia to Gades took hardly a week and still less from Ostia to Tarraco (Tarragona) whereas it took three weeks to go to Alexandria of Egypt. Therefore, it responded to the logic of

---

2. In Galatians 1:17, Paul does not state the purpose of his journey to Arabia. Since in Galatians 4:25, he refers to "Mount Sinai in Arabia," it can be supposed that his intention was to relive the spiritual experience of Moses and Elijah. Like them and like Jesus, he would have started his ministry with a desert experience. However, if Paul intended to evoke the Sinai, he would have done it more explicitly. Moreover, since, at the time of Paul, "Arabia" included the land from Damascus to Petra, exegetes are of the opinion that it was his first mission field. This is confirmed by the humoristic allusion to the escape from Damascus hidden in a basket (2 Cor. 11:32). The earliest Pauline ministry must have been in the surroundings of Damascus where he met with the opposition of king Aretas of Petra, in "Arabia."

the mission to the nations to push to the *fines terrae*, the end of the world then known in the West. Could Paul realize his project? Texts are silent about it. At any rate, Paul's mission horizon extended up to the Atlantic Ocean.

Pauline Geography: Scope and Limitations

However, extensive as it was, the mission field covered by the Apostle did not embrace the four corners of the horizon. It would be an anachronism to compare it with the geography we know today. But we can at least compare it with the vast vistas presented for instance in the book of Esther. The story takes place in Susa, the capital of the great king "who reigned from India to Ethiopia" (Est. 1:1). The campaigns of Alexander had also contributed to enlarge the geographical horizon of the Hellenistic world up to India. In the days of Paul, the *Res Gestae Divi Augusti*, or Acts of Augustus, gave a general idea of the geographical field embraced by a citizen of the Roman Empire. From the Danube in the north till the upper reaches of the Nile in the south and from Spain in the west to India in the east, it was a vast world map that the mausoleum of Augustus presented to the visitors. Even before he came to Rome, Paul could have read the inscription at Pisidian Antioch or in any other town where it had been copied. Anyway, as an educated citizen of the Mediterranean world, he could not be ignorant of the existence of these countries. If he turned toward Illyricum and not Egypt, toward Spain and not India, it could not be due to lack of awareness. Pauline strategy left aside two main major directions, the eastern one toward Babylonia and the other Asian "satrapies," and the southern one toward Egypt and Africa. These were not only geographical directions; they were also theological loci, given the importance of Egypt and Babylon in the history of Israel and in its faith in a saving God.

These are the major directions found in the map of the Diaspora given by Philo in the text quoted above. This text reflects the world vision entertained by a Jew of the first century CE and consequently by young Rabbi Saul. The Diaspora of Philo went far beyond the western framework of the Pauline mission. Philo and

Paul converge on Phoenicia, Syria, Cilicia, Asia Minor, Macedonia, Corinth, Cyprus, and Crete. But, as against the Pauline geography, the list of Philo does not extend westward (Illyricum and Spain) while, on the other hand, it covers the two main areas absent from the Pauline field, Asia and Africa.

The long and short is that the geography of Paul's apostolate does not cover the whole range of the Roman Empire. It is turned towards the West and bypasses two main directions of the history of Israel and of the spread of the Diaspora toward Asia and Africa. This major trend must be considered to assess the vast scope and the limitations of the mission field of the "Apostle to the Nations" and perceive its significance.

"We to the Gentiles, They to the Circumcision" (Galatians 2:9)

How then are we to understand the apostolic approach, characterized as it was by a vast outlook and a perspective limited to the West?

"Apostle to the Nations:" Which Nations?

We must first note that the word "nations" (*ethnē* in Greek), in the biblical context, has a precise signification. It translates the Hebrew word *go'im* which refers to pagan people as opposed to the People of God (*laos* in Greek, *'am* in Hebrew). It has a specific religious connotation as it refers to all those who are not marked by circumcision as members of the People of the Promises made to Abraham and of the Covenant bestowed to Moses. The connotation can be negative when the nations are represented by Egyptian oppression, Canaanite threats, the Babylonian captivity, or the persecutions of Antiochus Epiphanes. The attitude is more open toward the "Pagan Saints of the Old Testament,"[3] like the queen of Saba (1 Kgs. 10:1–13), Naaman the Syrian (2 Kgs.

---

3. Cf. J. Daniélou, *Holy Pagans of the Old Testament* (London: Longmans, Green & Co., 1957).

5:1–23), Cyrus the Persian king, "the shepherd, the anointed" (Isa. 44:28–45:1), and all the nations who will go up in peace to Jerusalem (Isa. 2:2–5) and whom God will recognize as children of Zion (Ps. 87). However, whether it is to despise them or to admire the grace of God bestowed on them, the nations are defined as "not my people" (Hos. 2:25), the "others." It is this otherness that Paul will commute into shared identity in Christ Jesus (Gal. 3:28). Therefore, the word "nations" does not connote absolute geographical universalism. When Paul calls himself "Apostle to the Nations," he does not claim to be missionary to the whole world. He specifies that his vocation sends him to the *go'im*, to those who do not belong to the people of Israel.

The Jerusalem Assembly (Galatians 2:1–10)

What then will be the field of the *go'im* entrusted to Paul? This was one of the main questions debated at the Jerusalem Assembly as reported in Galatians 2:1–10. The debate started with the theological problem of circumcision and thereby of submission to the Law. Then the argument moved to the specificity of Paul's apostolate to conclude with an allotment of the respective spheres of influence assigned to Paul and to the others.

> When they saw that I had been entrusted with the gospel to the uncircumcised, just as Peter had been entrusted with the gospel to the circumcised (for he who worked through Peter for his apostolic ministry to the circumcised worked also through me for mine to the Gentiles), and when James and Cephas and John, who seemed to be pillars, perceived the grace that was given to me, they gave the right hand of fellowship to Barnabas and me, that we should *be*[4] to the Gentiles and they to the circumcised. (Gal. 2:7–9)

How are we to understand this division: "we to the Gentiles, they to the circumcised"? The text has been interpreted in dif-

---

4. Translation modified to leave open the discussion on the implicit verb.

ferent ways.[5] At first a grammatical problem arises: the original text has no verb that would qualify the action. It just says: "*we to, they to*." Which is the implied verb? Should we understand "*going* to the Gentiles/to the circumcision" or "*address* the Gentiles/circumcision"? Moreover, does the division of responsibility concern *individual* Gentiles and circumcised Jews or collectively *the world of the Gentiles* and *the Jewish world*? Two translations are possible: "we would *go* to the Gentiles/circumcision" or "we would *address* only Gentiles/circumcision." Did the Jerusalem Assembly intend a *geographical* allotment of mission responsibilities sending Paul and the others in different areas? Or did it think of an *ethnic* division restricting the respective ministries to particular individuals or groups? In anachronistic terms, we could speak of territorial or personal jurisdiction.

If we go by the ethnic division, Paul would have been barred from announcing the Good News to Jews, who would have remained Peter's exclusive preserve whereas Peter and the others should henceforth avoid carefully resuming the initiative reported in Acts 10 to address such Gentiles as Cornelius and his family. This interpretation denies any historical value to the book of Acts according to which, when Paul enters a town, he goes first to its Jewish community. So it is in Cyprus (Acts 13:5–6), Pisidian Antioch (Acts 13:14–43), Iconium (Acts 14:1), Philippi (Acts 16:13), Thessalonica (Acts 17:1–2), Berea (Acts 17:10), Corinth (Acts 18:1–4), and finally Rome (Acts 28:16–27). This systematic construction may possibly reflect the stress that Lukan theology laid on the priority of Israel. Luke may have schematized his narrative. Yet, on the whole, the priority given to Israel tallies, as we have seen, with Paul's strategy based on the privileges granted to the people of Israel. In practice, Paul does not turn his back on his people: "To the Jews I became as a Jew, in order to win Jews. To those under the Law I became as one under the Law (though

---

5. I have treated the question more elaborately in *L'apôtre des nations? Paul et la stratégie missionnaire des églises apostoliques* (LD 184; Paris: Cerf, 2001).

not being myself under the Law) that I might win those under the Law" (1 Cor. 9:20). Later on, treating again the question of meat offered to idols, he expresses the concern "to give no offense to Jews or to Greeks or to the church of God" (1 Cor. 10:32). He counts a number of Jews among his collaborators, Prisca and Aquilas, Aristoboulos, Maria, Andronicus as well as Herodion, Lucius, Jason, and Sosipatros, "his relatives" (Rom. 16:3–21). The collection for the poor of Jerusalem, a recurring topic of his letters, reveals his attachment to the mother church (1 Cor. 16:1–4; 2 Cor. 8–9; Rom. 15:25–32; Gal. 2:10). The fact itself of the letter to Romans contradicts the ethnic interpretation. Among the Roman Christians, those of Jewish origin constituted an important element; they might even have been a majority. Yet Paul addresses them unhesitatingly.

Consequently, many commentators have recourse to the geographic interpretation. But, for many of them, the area of the "circumcision" was limited to Palestine.[6] The Twelve would have confined themselves to a minuscule province leaving the vast world to Paul. Evidently it would be an awkward compromise, "nothing less than an absurdity."[7] Anyway the text that follows in Galatians 2:11 shows that Peter did not intend to remain confined in Palestine since he is found in Antioch in a conflicting situation with Paul. Also and mostly, this interpretation presumes, as an author puts it, that Paul and Peter lacked breadth of vision and overlooked the Jews of the Diaspora, apparently unaware that there were more Jews in Egypt than in Palestine.[8] Can such a narrow-mindedness be presumed in a man issued from the Diaspora of Tarsus? Philo and the list of the nations present in Jerusalem for the feast of Pentecost according to Acts 2:9–11 prove that

---

6. Thus Fridrichsen who sees the mission divided into two well-defined geographical zones, Palestine on one side, and the world at large apart from Palestine on the other (*The Apostle and His Message* [Uppsala: University Press, 1947], 12).

7. J. Bligh, *Galatians* (London: St. Paul's, 1969), 168.

8. E. P. Sanders, *Paul, the Law and the Jewish People* (Philadelphia: Fortress, 1983), 189.

the Diaspora was very much in the mind of the average Jew of the first century CE.

Actually, to understand the decision of the Jerusalem Assembly, this Diaspora must be considered. It was important in the East and in Africa. It covered a vast area. From Egypt, it had gone up the Nile valley, was present in Elephantine, near Aswan, and, across Sudan, had reached Ethiopia. Acts presents the emblematic figure of a senior Ethiopian official, a fervent proselyte, faithful to the Jerusalem pilgrimage, and an avid reader of the Scriptures. The importance of the Diaspora was not only geographical and statistical; it was also sociocultural. The presence of a block of a million Jews out of a total population of seven million in Egypt and of an equal number in the Parthian Empire could not but exercise an influence on the collective mentality of those countries. In the East, toward Asia, as well as in the South, toward Africa, Judaism was part of the sociocultural landscape. It was admired or feared, acknowledged or rejected, but it was known and it impressed. The influence could be deliberately entertained by the likes of Philo, Aristoboulos, or Artapan. It could as well be diffused and unconsciously felt due to the very fact of its massive presence and of its vigorous sense of identity. Belonging to the world in which it lived, the Judaism of the Diaspora had become a part of the local culture and challenged it by the witness it gave of its monotheism and moral rectitude.

Coexistence induces a kind of connivance, and a common language issued from the shared background. When cultural backgrounds differ, a common language is missing. For instance, when Paul in Athens speaks of the Resurrection in Acts 17:22–23, the communication with the Athenians is broken. For them, the concept of a Resurrection from the dead is an absurdity that makes dialogue impossible. Some jeer; others more politely put off the matter to another day and the case is dismissed. We can presume that the reaction would have been different in Alexandria. The myth of Isis and Osiris subsisted in the Egyptian soul. Moreover, the local population was acquainted with the Jews, their beliefs and messianic expectations. Alexandria was as much an idolater as Athens, if not more. But it was familiar with the Jewish faith. As Acts reports, "From ancient generations Moses has had in every city those who proclaim him, for he is read every Sabbath in the synagogues" (Acts 15:21). The Jerusalem Assembly could presume that even Christians issued from paganism were sufficiently aware of the Jewish Law not to take amiss the few food restrictions and matrimonial regulations that Jews were required to observe. It was understood that synagogal preaching resounded beyond the walls of the synagogue.[9] Therefore the decision of the Assembly concerning the "circumcision" referred to this vast part of the world impacted by an effective presence of Judaism and by its influence. It went far beyond the small Palestinian province.[10]

This sociocultural presence of Judaism had no equivalent in the West. After the disastrous destruction of Jerusalem by the Roman legions of Titus in 70 CE, the Jewish population will be scattered all over the Roman Empire, especially through the slave market. But, before 70 CE, apart from the eastern façade of the Mediterranean Sea and cosmopolitan Rome, Jewish presence was minimal and even non-existent in northern Italy, Gaul, Spain, Germany, not to speak of the "barbarian tribes" north of the Danube. Even in Athens, Acts makes no mention of a synagogue. At Philippi, Jews were not enough to constitute the *minyan*, the minimum of participants required for a synagogal gathering: Paul could only meet a few women gathered on a brookside. In the West, before 70 CE, Judaism had no sociocultural presence. The Latin world had no Philo and nothing corresponding to Alexandrian Hellenistic Judaism. It had no counterpart to the Septuagint in Latin. The old Latin translation of the Bible (*Vetus*

---

9. This situation can be compared with the influence of Christianity on society in India, especially in the south where, in Kerala, the Christian population reaches 18 percent of the total population.

10. Subsequently, along with the growth of Christianity in the West, it will develop rapidly in what will become the Syriac, Coptic, Abyssinian churches. They are already flourishing in the second century. The ground had been prepared by the Diaspora.

Latina) will be a product of Christianity. Seen from Jerusalem, before 70 CE, the Western world, deprived of Jewish presence and influence was indeed the world of the *go'im*, the pagan world of the nations. This is what Paul means when he calls himself the "Apostle of the Nations." But "Peter, James and John considered as pillars" (Gal. 2:9) are entrusted with the world of the "circumcision," which extends far beyond Palestine. It is the entire East and South where the gospel will step in the path already opened by Israel.

In the division proposed in Jerusalem, the "nations" and the "circumcision" are perceived as two blocks defined respectively by the presence or the absence of Judaism, of its religious and cultural influence. The one is the totality of the countries where "Moses has had in every city those who proclaim him, for he is read every Sabbath in the synagogues" (Acts 15:21); the other one is deprived of this privilege. As a matter of fact, it happens that the block of the nations happens to be in Europe, in what the List of the Nations in Genesis 10 calls the domain of Japhet (Gen. 10:2–5) and that the other block extends east and south to the countries descending from Shem and Ham (Gen. 10:5–31). The division is geographical, but what determines it is not geography but the influence of Judaism. The geographical setting is not constitutive.[11] When assigning the zones of apostolic responsibility, the Jerusalem Assembly did not consult a biblical atlas. It just took note of the existence of two blocks imbued or not with Jewish influence. This is what determined the dividing line.[12]

The field assigned to Paul is not larger than that of the "circumcision." Its greatness is not a matter of mileage. It comes from the magnitude of the challenge that the Apostle will have

---

11. As proposed by J. M. Scott, *Paul and the Nations: The Old Testament and Jewish Background of Paul's Mission to the Nations with Special Reference to the Destination of Galatians* (WUNT 84; Tübingen: Mohr Siebeck, 1995), 6–54.

12. So, at the time of the "cold war," the blocks of East and West were so called on account of their geographical position. Yet it was not geography but ideology and political system which identified them.

to face. He will have to enter an unmarked field, where he cannot rely on any support, either religious or sociocultural. What will be the theological foundations, the structures, the ways of life, and the ethics that he will have to propose to the new *ekklēsiai* launched in the foreign world of the nations? What will be the attitude that they will be expected to assume toward "the outsiders" (1 Thess. 4:12; 1 Cor. 5:12)? To all these questions, Paul will answer with a creativeness, a boldness, but also a practical sense inspired by the Spirit. Mostly he will keep to his fundamental objective, the gathering of the nations in the eschatological times inaugurated by the Resurrection of Christ, and it is the "power of the Resurrection" that will animate the dynamism of this mission to the nations.

As for the block of the "circumcision," it is of no lesser importance. Not only will its field of apostolate be at least as extensive as that of the Apostle to the Nations, but also its theological significance will be predominant. In the world of the Dispersion of Israel, it will continue to carry the essential vocation of the Chosen People "to whom belong the adoption, the glory, the covenants, the giving of the Law, the worship, and the promises, to whom belong the patriarchs, and from whose race, according to the flesh, is the Christ who is God over all, blessed forever" (Rom. 9:4–5). The mission of the "pillars" is not a timid first attempt that would prepare Paul's soaring flight of missionary zeal. It constitutes the foundation, and, as such, it belongs fittingly to the pillars on whom will rest the universalistic development of the divine project.

Other Mission Fields. Other Mission Models

The decisions of the Jerusalem Assembly kept open the way for a pluralism of mission fields. The towering personality of Paul and the interest shown by Luke, his disciple, have resulted in a predominant Pauline part in the Christian canon.[13] This dispropor-

---

13. To get a rough idea, we may compare the number of pages devoted to Paul in an edition of the ESV (18 pages in double column for the Pauline

tion could obliterate the other mission drives that have developed in other areas, in other contexts, and on other bases. It makes it all the more important to take note of these other mission paths hinted at in the New Testament.[14]

Paul himself invites us to do it by the attitude he takes toward Apollos in 1 Corinthians. He says little about this missionary whom he met in Corinth and about whom the community had begun to split. At least he mentions that Apollos belonged to another mission current (1 Cor. 1:12), which he recognizes as equally respectable (1 Cor. 3:5, 22; 4:6). At the end of the letter, he encourages his rival to come to Corinth (1 Cor. 16:11). According to Acts, Apollos came from the Alexandrian Christian community (Acts 18:24; 19:11). Therefore, he represented another type of evangelization spreading in the wake of the Egyptian Diaspora. Paul and Apollos exemplify two models of apostolic mission that coexist in mutual respect.

We can only presume the type of evangelization adopted by the mission to the "circumcision." Since it was addressed to a Jewish milieu, it would have adopted the model of the Diaspora missionary dynamism that was based on the community witness. It was collective rather than stemming from the imposing personality of the founder. An example of this pluralistic form of the mission thrust can be found in Acts 2. It narrates the foundational Pentecostal event. The Spirit comes down on the gathered community (Acts 2:1, 4; cf. 1:14–15), and not only on the Twelve as too often presumed by customary Christian iconography. Therefore, it is the Spirit and its power that will be manifested in various ways on that day and throughout history. This power appears in the

---

section of Acts and 62 pages for the Pauline corpus) with the Johannine corpus (22 pages for John and 5 pages for the Johannine epistles). The ratio is 80:27. The four Gospels take a hundred pages. Paul alone almost equals the four Gospels together.

14. I have developed the point in *Unity and Plurality: Mission in the Bible* (New York: Orbis Books, 1992). For a development of this pluralism in the history of the mission, see D. J. Bosch, *Transforming Mission: Paradigm Shifts in Mission Theology* (New York: Orbis Books, 1991).

proclamation of the Good News by Peter. It is effective as three thousand souls receive the word and are baptized (Acts 2:14–41). But then, it is the turn of the community to relay the power of the Spirit by the witness of a lived faith, of an effective communion, of an ardent prayer in the Temple and at home. The outcome equals that of Peter's discourse: "the Lord added to their number day by day those who were being saved" (Acts 2:47). In this chapter, under the same impulse of the Holy Spirit, Peter represents the direct proclamation of the gospel whereas the witness of the community, in the manner of the Diaspora, expresses the new life of those who, in faith, "are being saved."

The two ways of evangelization are complementary. They converge in the ministry of Paul. He proclaims the crucified Messiah and the Risen Lord. But his proclamation intends to bring about the People of the new times, the image of which is shown by the *ekklēsia*, "shining as light in the world, holding fast to the word of life" (Phil. 2:15–16).

Conclusion

Paul's mission needs to be viewed in the larger context of the various forms of the apostolic field. The Jerusalem Assembly was not lacking in breadth of vision. It embraced a universalistic perspective as it formulated an agreement on the respective competences of Paul and of the others. To Paul was assigned the ministry to the nations, of the pagan world, and so practically the western part of the Roman Empire. It was an awesome challenge that the Apostle faced with unique zeal and creative genius. But the other face of universalism was represented by the apostolic field of the "circumcision," of the part of the world where the proclamation of the gospel could lean on the presence and the faith of the Jewish people. Its history is not as well known, as there was no Luke to describe it. But its fruits are manifest in the flourishing of the Eastern and Coptic churches from the early days of Christian antiquity.

So, Paul did not view himself in isolation as if he had been the unique *Apostle*.

When one says, "I follow Paul," and another, "I follow Apollos," are you not being merely human? What then is Apollos? What is Paul? Servants through whom you believed, as the Lord assigned to each. I planted, Apollos watered, but God gave the growth. So, neither he who plants nor he who waters is anything, but only God who gives the growth. He who plants and he who waters are one, and each will receive his wages according to his labor. For we are God's fellow workers. (1 Cor. 3:4–9)

Paul does not stand on a pedestal. He does not claim a mission monopoly. The greatness of his mission does not induce pride. He knows he is only a servant of God, of Christ, and of his communities: "Let no one boast in men. For all things are yours, whether Paul or Apollos or Cephas or the world or life or death or the present or the future. All are yours, and you are Christ's, and Christ is God's" (1 Cor. 3:21–23).

A Pluralistic Mission

Mission is spelled out in the plural. This is illustrated by the conclusion of the four Gospels. They all conclude with a mission mandate. The disciples are entrusted with the task of resuming the messianic work of Jesus. Christology is relayed by an ecclesiology of the church in mission. The mission of the church extends the messianic mission of Jesus, and reciprocally, the mission of the church is carried by the power of his Resurrection. But, on the basis of this fundamental convergence, the Gospels differ on the ways in which this mission is accomplished.

The Gospel of Matthew presents a mission that "makes disciples." The term evokes the rabbinical model according to which the learned scribe transmits to his disciples the tradition that he has received and its interpretation. It corresponds to the image, given by the Gospel, of Jesus sitting on the mountain of the new Sinai, solemnly "opening his mouth" (Matt. 5:1–2) to give a teaching that will extend over three chapters (Matt. 5–7). Like the scribes, Jesus starts with the Law to proceed with its interpretation, a very radical one indeed. The mission that "makes disciples" will follow the same model of the "scribe well trained for the kingdom of heaven . . . who brings out of his treasure what is new and what is old" (Matt. 13:52). This model corresponds to the Jewish Christian milieu to which the first Gospel is addressed. It corresponds also to the date of composition of the Gospel. It is commonly accepted to belong to a time when, after the first proclamation of the Good News, the need was felt for a fuller understanding of faith to adapt it to ongoing times.

In Luke-Acts, the mission thrust takes the form of "witness." "You shall be my witnesses" (Luke 24:48; cf. Acts 1:8). What witness means is exemplified by the picture of the ideal community of the early days in Acts 2:42–47. This example of brotherhood united in listening to the apostolic teaching, in prayer, in the "breaking of the bread," and in sharing of goods is as eloquent as vocal proclamation. This image illustrates a mission drawing to faith through its enlightening influence. A world divided between rich and poor, mighty and downtrodden, felt attracted by a community united in faith and sharing "one heart and one soul" (Acts 4:32).

The Gospel of John deepens this theme of unity as the source of dynamism of the mission. This unity stems from the heart of the Trinity. It is the manifestation of the divine glory, and it transmits its irradiation to the world. "May they all be one, just as you, Father, are in me, and I in you, that they also may be in us, so that the world may believe that you have sent me. The glory that you have given me I have given to them, that they may be one even as we are one, I in them and you in me, that they may become perfectly one, so that the world may know that you sent me and loved them even as you loved me" (John 17:21–23). Sent on their mission, the disciples will extend the mission of the Son. Their mission will be impelled by the power of the Spirit in the apocalyptic combat for peace against the sin of the world (John 20:21–23).

As for the mission mandate in the long ending of Mark, it presents the model mission of vocal proclamation: "Go into the whole world and proclaim the gospel to the whole creation" (Mark 16:15). But the reference to "the whole world" has done away with the distinction between the nations and the circumcision. The mission is now one-sided. This suggests a rather late period when the success of the gospel to the Gentiles has come to blanket the parallel mission to Israel.

Mission of proclamation, teaching mission, witnessing mission, mission issuing from the heart of the Trinity: the various Gospels evoke various mission models adapted to various times and settings. This pluralism of mission models will continue in the history of missions as, through the centuries, they encounter new worlds.

9

Mission Methods

Global strategy is to be applied in ground tactics. This applies to mission practice and so it was for Paul. He took concrete steps to translate his vast project of extension of Israel to the nations. The methods that he used were his own, depending on his personality and his cultural background. They were also conditioned by the cultural and sociopolitical environment. We shall now consider the Apostle's methods under three angles: his travels, his interventions by word and deed, and his letters.

Traveling

Paul had been entrusted with a vast field. From Jerusalem to Illyricum and Rome, possibly even Spain, long was the way he trod.

Paul on the Way

The geography of Paul's journeys reflects the strategy explained above. It is turned westward, toward the world of the "nations." We do not know whether he realized his Spanish project. Aiming at Spain was a logical consequence of his strategy since Spain was the extreme edge, the *finis terrae* of the pagan West. The other extremity in the East, India, did not fall within the field assigned to him.

In this vast setting, Paul did not hang around villages. His ministry focused on cities and even mostly on the important ones: Antioch, Ephesus, Thessalonica, Philippi, Athens, Corinth, and Rome. The Pauline space is urban. We shall see below the cultural consequences. His travels were facilitated by the *Pax Romana*, the orderly situation that reigned from the Tigris River to the Atlantic Ocean, unifying East and West. This vast unification simplified the apostolic journeys. A small bag containing a few *aurei* or *denarii* was as good as a passport. From Syrian Antioch to Iberian Tarragona and up to the Pillars of Hercules no national border could block the apostolic ways.

The network of Roman roads materialized the unity of the empire and bolstered it. The *Via Egnatia* particularly was the central highway of Paul's mission. Starting from Byzantium, it ran through Macedonia and, across Illyricum; it reached the Adriatic harbors of Apollonia and Dyrrachium from where a short sail across the Strait of Otranto touched Brindisi and the *Via Appia,* which went straight to Rome. Military stations, set at regular intervals along the way, maintained security, though their protection might not have been totally effective since Paul will mention "dangers from brigands" (2 Cor. 11:26).

In spite of these facilities, traveling was arduous. We can imagine Paul, hunched up in his *chlamys* or his *paenula*, progressing on foot or on the back of an ass, under freezing rain or burning sun. Occasionally, he could find a place in the midst of sundry wares on a *benna* or chariot, or better, if he could afford it and if it was available, he could sit in a *raeda*, a four-wheeled carriage. At night, unless he could find someone to whom he would have been recommended, he had to depend on the dubious comfort of lodgings swarming with animal vermin and rough humans.

Sea journeys were often preferred. They were faster but ran their own risks. Pirates had long infested the Mediterranean Sea. Well organized, they had long held fast against the Roman navy. It was only in 67 BCE that Pompey defeated them in a three-month campaign. In the list of his trials in 2 Corinthians 11:23–27, Paul does not refer to piracy. But conditions on board were not better than on land. According to Acts 27:37, the ship that took Paul to Rome had 273 persons on board. Added to the cargo, the crowding must have been quite excruciating. Storms were frequent in the Mediterranean Sea and they could end in a shipwreck. Paul states that it happened thrice to him (2 Cor. 11:24). On the contrary, winds would drop, and the ship would stay becalmed under a scorching sun.

A fanatical opposition added to those natural mishaps. The message of the Apostle was disturbing. It challenged local cults as well as the deification of imperial authority. It also shook the fragile balance established between Jewish communities and Greco-Roman society. In 2 Corinthians 11:23–27, Paul himself provides the best summary of the trials and tribulations he encountered:

> great labors, . . . imprisonments, . . . countless beatings, and often near death.
> Five times I received at the hands of the Jews the forty lashes less one.
> Three times I was beaten with rods.
> Once I was stoned.
> Three times I was shipwrecked;
> a night and a day I was adrift at sea;
> on frequent journeys,
> in danger from rivers, danger from robbers,
> danger from my own people, danger from Gentiles,
> danger in the city, danger in the wilderness, danger at sea,
> danger from false brothers,
> in toil and hardship, through many a sleepless night,
> in hunger and thirst, often without food, in cold and exposure. (2 Cor. 11:23–27)

Luke has been suspected of having written as a novel writer rather than as a historian and of having given free way to his imagination. It is the opposite; he could rather be blamed for lack of imagination. But for the last captivity journey, he does not expound the risks and hassles of Paul's journeys; he does not dwell on the weariness, hunger, thirst of the exhausted traveler, makes no reference to attacks by brigands. He reports only one shipwreck out of the three and does not describe the dramatic "night and day adrift at sea." He mentions only one scourging (Acts 16:22–24), but the matter ends with humble apologies from the authorities (Acts 16:39). In another circumstance, Paul will prevail of his title as Roman citizen to escape the whip (Acts 22:24–26). On the basis of the outline given by Paul in 2 Corinthians 11:23–27, a novelist could have produced a much more colorful story than Acts. If Paul had written his memoirs, they would have been quite fascinating.

Financing[1]

As soon as he landed in Greece, Paul adopted the principle of financial autonomy: "you remember, brothers, our labor and toil: we worked night and day, that we might not be a burden to any of you, while we proclaimed to you the gospel of God" (1 Thess. 2:9–10). In that he followed Jewish tradition, which, faithful to the command of Genesis 1:28, respected manual labor. Scribes showed the example by exercising manual professions. Amidst his problems with the Corinthians, he gloried in the fact that he was not a burden to them (1 Cor. 4:12; 9:6, 14–15; 2 Cor. 11:7–10; 12:13–18; cf. 2 Thess. 3:7–8; Acts 18:3; 20:33–35).

The paltry wages of his manual work sufficed to meet his daily needs. But they were not enough to subsidize his traveling. For the disciples of Jesus, who had only to go round a few Galilean villages, money was no matter; day-to-day hospitality was enough. But the case was different when the Apostle had to travel the length and breadth of Roman roads, get equipment for the journey, meet traveling expenses in caravans or on ship, pay tolls or any other local taxes, and settle lodging bills. His letters show that, without being a cause of worries, the financing of apostolic campaigns had to be considered. He is straightforward about it when thanking the Philippians for their support:

> I rejoiced in the Lord greatly that now at length you have revived your concern for me. You were indeed concerned for me, but you had no opportunity. Not that I am speaking of being in need, for I have learned in whatever situation

---

1. Cf. C. Tassin, *L'apôtre Paul: Un autoportrait* (Paris: Desclée de Brouwer, 2009), 191–234.

I am to be content. I know how to be brought low, and I
know how to abound. In any and every circumstance, I have
learned the secret of facing plenty and hunger, abundance
and need. I can do all things through him who strengthens
me. Yet it was kind of you to share my trouble. And you
Philippians yourselves know that in the beginning of the
gospel, when I left Macedonia, no church entered into partnership with me in giving and receiving, except you only.
Even in Thessalonica you sent me help for my needs once
and again. Not that I seek the gift, but I seek the fruit that
increases to your credit. I have received full payment, and
more. I am well supplied, having received from Epaphrodi-
tus the gifts you sent, a fragrant offering, a sacrifice acceptable and pleasing to God. (Phil. 4:10–18)

He mentions "an account of giving and receiving" (Phil. 4:15).[2]
Commentators tend to spiritualize the meaning of this "account."
It would be the exchange between the spiritual goods brought by
the Apostle and the financial help provided by the community.[3]
But the obvious meaning of the text seems to be rather that the
Philippians maintained an account in support of the Pauline mission.[4] Similarly, if he tells the Romans about his Spanish project,
it is in order to get their support: "I hope to see you in passing as
I go to Spain and to be sent on my way there by you, after I have
enjoyed being with you for a time" (Rom. 15:24). He did not only
recommend his mission to their prayer. He also appealed to their
financial help, their knowledge of the western part of the empire
and the contacts they could have over there. He wrote the letter
from Corinth; from there to the shores of the Atlantic Ocean, the

---

2. NAB translation that renders better the meaning of the text.

3. "Between the apostle and community there is a reciprocal relation.
The community shares in the spiritual gifts of the apostle and it grants him
a share in its own material goods" (F. Hauck, art. *koinos*, *TDNT*, 3:808).

4. "As in Gal 6:6 (and possibly in Rom 15:27) the verb refers to a financial participation" (J. N. Aletti, *Epître aux Philippiens* [EB 45; Paris: Gabalda, 2005], 309).

road was long and the sea journey perilous. He could not undertake such a journey all by himself, without any guide. He also needed an interpreter in parts of the world where Greek was not spoken. A budget had to be prepared. If he wrote such a lengthy letter to the Romans, it is, among other reasons, that he expected much from them.

A Pauline Odyssey?

The Acts of the Apostles gives a detailed account of Paul's apostolic journeys. The captivity journey especially is characterized by amazing precision concerning the stages and the hazardous sailing conditions in the Mediterranean sea as it accumulates geographical, climactic, topographical, and maritime precisions.[5] In that respect, the Acts have been compared with the travelogues, as popular in antiquity as they are today. They were the object of an abundant literature in the form of myths, like the *Odyssey* or the Myth of the Golden Fleece, of novels like Petronius's *Satiricon*, or of exploration reports like the *Periplus of the Eritrean Sea,* which reached India.[6] Consequently, Acts has been considered as a kind of Christian *Odyssey*. The comparison may be helpful. However, it overlooks an essential difference. The ancient *peripli* are stories that bring the hero back home. The word *periplus* itself suggests circular journeys. Ulysses goes back to Ithaka. But for Peter and Paul, there is no return home. Acts tells a one-way story. It does not relate a *periplus*, a return to the starting point. It moves forward toward a set goal. It aims at a beyondness, like Jesus "setting his face to go to Jerusalem when the days drew near to him to be taken up" (Luke 9:51). At the image of Jesus, Acts reports the ascensional way outlined by the

---

5. Cf. the elaborate study of Ch. Reynier, *Paul de Tarse en Méditerranée: Recherches autour de la navigation dans l'antiquité (Ac 27–28,16)* (LD 206; Paris: Cerf, 2006).

6. Cf. D. Marguerat, "Travels and Travelers," in *The First Christian Historian: Writing the Acts of the Apostles* (SNTSMS 121; Cambridge: Cambridge University Press, 2002), 231–56.

Risen One "from Jerusalem to all Judaea and Samaria, and till the ends of the earth" (Acts 1:8).

Peter initiates the move: From Jerusalem and Judaea (Acts 2–7), he goes to Samaria (Acts 8:1–40) and reaches the heart of the Roman presence when he meets the Roman centurion in Caesarea (Acts 9:32–11:18). Paul resumes and extends the journeys of Jesus and Peter. The conventional pattern of three "missionary journeys" wrongly projects the odyssean model into the biblical text. First, it unduly disconnects the captivity journey from the overall context of the book. Actually, it constitutes its summit. It is eminently a "missionary journey" as, in the context of a "passion," it takes the Apostle to Rome, the center of the pagan world.[7] The Pauline itinerary is not sectioned in discontinued circles. Through various ups and downs, setbacks and progresses, as befits a good plot, it progresses toward its goal when the Apostle "with complete assurance and without hindrance proclaimed the Kingdom of God and taught about the Lord Jesus Christ" (Acts 28:31).[8] It is not the end of the journey. Rome is not the "end of the earth" but the capital of the pagan world. It will be up to the reader to pursue the mission toward its eschatological fulfillment. As a major characteristic of the book, "the journey . . . exercises a structuring and unifying function in the plot of the book of Acts."[9]

As for the letters of Paul himself, they present his journeys from another angle. They suppose much journeying, in Galatia, at Philippi, Thessalonica, Corinth, Rome, and even possibly in Spain. To that extent, on the whole, they confirm the historicity of Acts. He describes his moves as going "from Jerusalem all the way round" (*en kyklō*, Rom. 15:19).[10] But this does not mean

---

7. Cf. L. Legrand, "St Paul in Acts: Triple or Single Missionary Journey?" *ITS* 55 (2018): 291–307.

8. Cf. D. Marguerat, "The Enigma of the End of Acts 28:16–31," in *The First Christian Historian*, 205–30.

9. D. Marguerat, "Travels and Travelers," in *The First Christian Historian*, 236.

10. "According to Chrysostom and his followers, the phrase must

that he viewed his traveling as another *Odyssey*. The "cycle" of the Pauline journeys did not bring him back to Jerusalem since it took him to Illyricum and made him, at least, dream of Spain. The ultimate goal of the journeys was rather the transcendent exaltation of the heavenly Jerusalem, the city of the free children of God (Gal. 4:26–27). On the other hand, Pauline itinerancy is no consistent progression toward a specified objective. The journeys of the Apostle do not exercise a "structuring function" in his ministry. Actually, the Apostle did not spend his missionary life on the roads or at sea. In addition to the time he lingered in jails, he spent two years in Ephesus (Acts 19:8, 10; 1 Cor. 16:8) and, from there, visited Corinth several times, where he stayed for a year and half according to Acts 18:11. We can fancy him shuttling to and fro between these two main centers of his apostolate. Crossing from one to the other was easy since the Cyclades islands provided seamarks or ports of call. Paul came back frequently to the communities that he had founded in Macedonia (1 Cor. 16:5). It was not enough to proclaim the *kerygma*, to present "the mystery of God . . . Jesus Christ and he crucified" (1 Cor. 2:1–2). Follow-up was needed to deepen and put the "message of the Cross" into practice. Paul uses the metaphor of weaning: he began feeding with milk until he could give solid food" (1 Cor. 3:2). The correspondence with the Corinthians illustrates the process. It recalls the initial *kerygma* of the Resurrection (chap. 15), of the Lord's Supper (1 Cor. 11:17–34), and mostly of the "word of the Cross" (1 Cor. 1:18–25). But it goes also into an initial canon law when it adopts the Torah of Leviticus 18:8, which prohibits marriage with one's mother-in-law under pain of excommunication (1 Cor. 5:1–5). Instead of taking a case to civil court, the Apostle proposes the internal jurisdiction (1 Cor. 6:1–11) that

---

be understood of journeys in different directions which Paul undertook between the two opposite points of Jerusalem in the South East and Illyricum in the North West. Instead of moving in a straight line, he went in a circuitous manner" (M.-J. Lagrange, *Épître aux Romains* [EB; Paris: Gabalda, 6th printing, 1950], 353).

will be further developed in Matthew 18:15–18. The celebration of the cult also raises problems. They will be answered by a kind of elementary liturgical *Ordo* concerning a ritual dress code for women (1 Cor. 11:1–16) and the good order to be observed during prayer meetings (1 Cor. 14:26–28), especially at the Lord's Supper (1 Cor. 11:23–29). Instructions are also given on the attitude to adopt on the occasion of meals that serve meat possibly coming from pagan sacrifices (chaps. 8–10). It all sounds like a course of pastoral theology on the way to handle tensions in communities.

Soon, elementary faith had to come to terms with daily life and its problems. The Apostle had to become a pastor. This followed the logic of his communitarian strategy. This pastoral aspect of Paul's ministry had to be noted to correct the image of a wandering knight or of the adventurer of the gospel. The mission model of the Apostle did not stop with "the propagation of faith." As we have seen, it went further and was more encompassing and collective. It tended to form communities gathered as *ekklēsia* through faith in the Good News. In this consisted the "structuring and unifying function" of the mission of the Apostle to the Nations.

The Proclamation

Initial Contact

"I did not at all shrink from telling you what was for your benefit, or from teaching you in public or in your homes. I earnestly bore witness for both Jews and Greeks to repentance before God and to faith in our Lord Jesus." "In public or in your homes . . . for both Jews and Greeks": it is in these terms that Paul summarizes his evangelizing methods, according to Acts 20:20–21. In other words, he never missed an opportunity to proclaim the Good News, and Acts reports many such instances.

Since the letters of Paul are addressed to communities, they hardly present any instance of witness given individually. We can only presume that long journeys provided many opportunities of personal meetings. We get at least an instance of private encounter in the letter sent to Philemon. Though it is not a case of first contact, the short note gives an idea of the kind of heart-to-heart conversation that the Apostle could entertain. We are privy to a friendly exchange on a delicate matter that could have led to misunderstanding. Since his slave Onesimus had run away, Philemon could consider that, having been wronged, he had a claim to restitution and was entitled to give adequate chastisement. Paul asks him to forgo his rights and to open his heart in a spirit of faith. The short message makes delightful reading. Paul shifts from praise to irony, from the position of poor old man in jail to that of the master entitled to gratitude. Addressing a businessman, he speaks the language of accounting to reverse its significance. "A masterpiece of tact and heart," the letter gives an idea of what could have been the apostolic exchanges along the road or at night in the lodgings.[11]

As regards proclaiming faith "in public," since the epistles address communities of believers, they tell us little about the early stages of evangelization. The case of the Galatians is all the more interesting. In his argument with the opponents, Paul evokes the way in which he came to contact the people of Galatia.

> You know that it was because of a physical illness that I originally preached the gospel to you, and you did not show disdain or contempt because of the trial caused you by my physical condition, but rather you received me as an angel of God, as Christ Jesus. Where now is that blessedness of yours? Indeed, I can testify to you that, if it had been possible, you would have torn out your eyes and given them to me. (Gal. 4:13–15)

Galatians were pagans (Gal. 4:8; 5:2–3; 6:12–13). Paul was an intruder, a total stranger. As a Jew, he came under suspicion. As a sick man, he was not attractive but rather troublesome. According to the popular mentality of those days, some evil spirit could be

---

11. M. Goguel quoted in the introduction to the letter in the French TOB translation.

suspected to be lurking in this ailing person. The normal reaction should have been "disdain or contempt." The power of the Good News overcame these problems. But the sickly apostle must have been also endowed with a remarkable capacity to attract attention; he was able to turn Galatians away from their initial repulsion to listen to the message and finally accept it. The letter proceeds displaying Paul's capacity to empathize with his neophytes and to relate with them in tender attachment: "my little children, for whom I am again in the anguish of childbirth until Christ is formed in you! I wish I could be present with you now and change my tone, for I am perplexed about you" (Gal. 4:19–20).

Apart from the Galatian case, we know little of the way in which the Apostle approached people. According to Acts, he did it by first working through the network of the Diaspora, at least where it existed. There is no reason why he would not have used it. His love for his people must have prompted him to give them the priority of the Good News. Even if they turned hostile, they would have entertained him, at least initially.

He could also benefit from the network of professional corporations. Coming from a family of weavers, according to Acts 18:3, he would have enjoyed the corporative solidarity of the textile profession. These bonds of solidarity helped him to establish contacts and, occasionally, to get room and board in some towns. In this way, according to Acts 16:14–15, he was received in Corinth by a dealer in purple goods and fellow textile industrialist. He even worked with them in one of their workshops (Acts 18:3–4). The letters do not give such particulars, but they make specific mention of Aquila and Priscilla, the owners of a workshop (1 Cor. 16:19; Rom. 16:3–4), as privileged members of the apostolic circle. The wages of his labor gave him financial independence and provided him with opportunities to relate with coworkers. We can only guess the way in which the workshop turned into a forum for the word of God. Whether it be by way of planned or occasional visits, the Apostle would never have missed a chance to speak of the Risen One. "By word or by deed," he had to proclaim the Good News.

"By Word"

According to his opponents, Paul lacked in oratory skill: "His letters are weighty and strong, but his bodily presence is weak, and
his speech of no account" (2 Cor. 10:10). The Jerusalem Bible has
a more picturesque translation: "when you see him in person, he
makes no impression, and his powers of speaking are negligible."
His adversaries would have referred to his short stature, but,
judging by the results, his speech was not "negligible." It could
touch mind and heart.

Certainly, he did not turn his message into a rhetorical exercise and did not vaunt "lofty speech or wisdom" (1 Cor. 2:1):

> I decided to know nothing among you except Jesus Christ
> and him crucified. And I was with you in weakness and in
> fear and much trembling, and my speech and my message
> were not in plausible words of wisdom, but in demonstra-
> tion of the Spirit and of power, that your faith might not
> rest in the wisdom of men but in the power of God. (1 Cor.
> 2:2–5)

However, the "power of the spirit" worked through oratory skills
that would have been the envy of professional rhetors. Paul knew
how to communicate his convictions forcefully. When a student in Tarsus, he would have received good literary training.
The "power of the Spirit" made use of these human inborn and
acquired capacities. The same passage that decries the wisdom of
the wise and claims to keep away from the prestige of eloquence
leads him to "display treasures of rhetorical skillfulness."[12] As a
commentator puts it, "Paradox: this passage which proclaims the
crucified Christ shows such literary qualities as to be compared
with the best pages of Demosthenes."[13]

Paul is sincere: his writings are no exercises in pedantic oratory.

---

12. M. Quesnel, *La première épître aux Corinthiens* (CBNT 7; Paris:
Cerf, 2018), 65.

13. P. de Surgy, *Les épîtres de Paul: I Corinthiens* (Paris: Bayard/Cen-
turion, 1996), 23.

His lively style stems spontaneously from the forcefulness of his thought. Yet his thought has been shaped by the lessons learned in Tarsus. His eloquence does not pursue school rhetoric. It arises from his fervor, but this fervor would have found another shape if the young student from Tarsus had not been trained in classics. His genius would have expressed itself in other forms had it been born in Persia, India, or China. Indeed, his style reflects the Tarsus background; it is the style of "no mean a city" (Acts 21:39), which, as seen above, was one of the intellectual centers of the Hellenistic world. His letters spontaneously reproduce the classical epistolary structure, though this structure gives way to creative originality. Like any Greco-Roman letter, they begin with a prologue giving the identity of the sender (*superscriptio*: "Paul and Timothy"), the addressee (*adscriptio*: "to the church . . .") and a greeting formula (*salutatio*: "grace and peace"). The argument of the letter follows the logical construction of Greco-Roman rhetoric. A report of the facts (*narratio*: cf. Gal. 1:6–2:15) is followed by a *propositio* announcing the leading theme (Gal. 2:16–21). Then comes the body of the letter proving the theme (*demonstratio*: Gal. 3:1–4:31) and concluding with an *exhortatio* (Gal. 5:1–6:10). Paul uses the stylistic devices of Greek rhetoric like chiasmus, paradox, personification or prosopopoeia, parallelism, antithesis, anacolutha, metaphor, metonymy, ellipse, oxymoron, gradation. He applies a variety of literary forms like diatribe, apostrophe, oratory interrogation, irony, allegory, parenesis.[14]

Paul's style is of the intellectual type. It tends more to argumentation than to parable. We cannot apply to him what was said of Jesus: "With many parables he spoke the word. . . . He did not speak to them without a parable" (Mark 4:33–34). When occasionally Paul takes to figurative language, the symbolic field is that of the cultured Hellenistic world: music (1 Cor. 14:7–8), athletics (1 Cor. 9:24–27), anatomy (1 Cor. 12:14–27), politics

---

14. Cf. S. E. Porter, "Paul of Tarsus and His Letters," in *Handbook of Classical Rhetoric in the Hellenistic Period* (ed. S. E. Porter; Leiden/New York: Brill, 1997), 533–86.

(Phil. 3:20; cf. Rom. 13:1–7). The style also reflects an urban background. Unlike in Jesus's language, agricultural images are rare and, if at all, ill fitting. In 1 Corinthians 3:6–9, the plant once sown and watered turns into a building. In Romans 11:17–18, the wild olive shoot is grafted onto the main trunk, which goes against sound horticulture. Unlike Jesus, Paul, a city man, does not live in harmony with nature from which he would draw his teaching. His allegories follow the logic of his ideas and not the course of nature. But this intellectual and urban style, with its qualities and limitations, was suited to the audience he intended to reach. The urban origin of the Apostle well matched the purpose intended by his strategy. It aimed at the great centers of the world of the nations. Paul spoke their language.

However, the man from Tarsus was also a Jew, first trained in the local synagogue and then in Jerusalem "at the feet of Gamaliel," for a more advanced rabbinical education (Acts 22:3). So, he is as expert and adept in rabbinical techniques as in classical rhetoric. Especially in letters addressed to communities having a substantial Jewish component, as in Rome, he speaks as a Christian rabbi. In the rabbinical way, he gathers texts that clarify each other (Rom. 4:3, 7–8; 9:25–29; 10:5, 20; 11:4–10). Large sections of the *demonstratio* follow the midrashic technique according to which a text or an episode of the Bible is applied to the present-day situation. In this way, in Galatians 3:6–29, the midrash of Abraham the believer illustrates the supremacy of faith. Faith as the way to freedom is explained by the midrash of the two spouses of Abraham: Hagar, the slave, symbolizes the enslavement to the Law, whereas Sarah, the free wife, represents the freedom of the Spirit (4:21–31). In Romans 5:12–21, the midrash of Adam develops the antithesis between Adam and Christ, sin and grace, life and death. The Jewish audience could but relish this rabbinical brilliance. As for the non-Jews, they could at least feel the charm of exoticism and admire the conclusion:

> For as many of you as were baptized into Christ have put on Christ. There is neither Jew nor Greek, there is neither

slave nor free, there is no male and female, for you are
all one in Christ Jesus. And if you are Christ's, then you
are Abraham's offspring, heirs according to promise. (Gal.
3:27–29)

"Jew with the Jews" and Greek with the Greeks: the Apostle to
the Nations knew how to adapt his language. He knew whom he
addressed, and he knew how to address them.

"By Deed"

Deeds go along with words, "by the power of signs and wonders,
by the power of the Spirit of God" (Rom. 15:19). According to
2 Corinthians 12:12, "the signs of a true apostle were performed
among you with utmost patience, with signs and wonders and
with mighty works." The Acts of the Apostles reports at length
the miracles performed from town to town: blinding of a magi-
cian in Cyprus (Acts 13:8–13), healing of a paralytic in Lystra
(Acts 14:8–10), miraculous liberation in Philippi (Acts 16:25–40),
resurrection of a youth in Troas (Acts 20:7–12), immunity to
snake bite in Malta (Acts 28:3–6). These miracles match those of
Peter in the first part of the book.

The epistles are more restrained about this miraculous activity. Unlike his biographer, Paul does not vaunt it. He hardly mentions it, and, when he does it, he seems to keep away from it as if
he were only an amazed observer. "Signs were performed among
you," he says. The verb is in the passive: "were performed." It is
not the Apostle who performed them; it is as though he had only
seen them happening and it was "among them," in the midst of
the community as though they had participated in the event as
much if not more than himself. The parallel text of Romans 15:18
states clearly who accomplished these wonders: it is "Christ who
accomplished through me . . . by the power of the Spirit." We are
brought back to the "power of his Resurrection," power of the
Spirit working in the community.

Paul will be more personally involved in the caritative activity
of the collection for the poor of Jerusalem, which he considers

to be a major component of his apostolate.[15] He comes back to it repeatedly (1 Cor. 16:1–4; 2 Cor. 8–9; Rom. 15:25–26). While endorsing the ministry to the non-Jews, the Jerusalem assembly had added a proviso: "to remember the poor (of Jerusalem)." Paul adds at once: "the very thing I was eager to do" (Gal. 2:10).[16] It is a project that seems to underlie the entire Pauline ministry. As soon as he began his ministry in Macedonia, in Thessalonica and Philippi, the new Christians responded generously to Paul's appeal (Phil. 4:10–18; 2 Cor. 8:1–5; 11:7–9). The Corinthians seem to be less forthcoming. After a first request in conclusion of 1 Corinthians 16:1–4, Titus has to be sent to kindle their zeal (2 Cor. 8:16, 23), and two long chapters back the plea (2 Cor. 8–9). Actually, they may constitute a separate letter sent to prompt them to open their hearts and their purse.

The Apostle runs the collection with the practical sense and the accounting meticulousness inherited from the family background. "We take this course so that no one should blame us about this generous gift that is being administered by us, for we aim at what is honorable not only in the Lord's sight but also in the sight of man" (2 Cor. 8:20–21). He gives practical advice: "On the first

---

15. Cf. K. F. Nickle, *The Collection: A Study in Paul's Strategy* (SBT; London: SCM, 1966); D. R. Hall, "St Paul and Famine Relief," *ET* 82 (1970): 309–11; L. Legrand, "'That We Remember the Poor' (Gal 2:10): The Conclusion of the Jerusalem Synod according to Gal 2:10," *ITS* 32 (1995): 161–73; *L'apôtre des nations?*, 97–110; J. Pathrapankal, "Apostolic Commitment and 'Remembering the Poor'. A Study in Gal 2:10," in T. Fornberg and D. Hellholm (eds.), *Texts and Contexts . . . in Honor of Lars Hartmann* (Oslo: Scandinavian University Press, 1995), 1001–18; C. Tassin, *L'apôtre Paul: Un autoportrait* (Paris: Desclée de Brouwer, 2009), 213–32; B. W. Longenecker, *Remember the Poor: Paul, Poverty and the Greco-Roman World* (Grand Rapids: Eerdmans, 2010).

16. The Greek verb used by Paul (*espoudasa* in the aorist) can be understood in two ways. Either: "what henceforth I have been eager to do": the concern for the poor would have been a response to the request of the Assembly. Or, as preferred in general by commentators, "what already I had been eager to do." It is not a matter of pleasing the assembly. It is rather a basic component of Paul's apostolate.

day of every week, each of you is to put something aside and store it up, as he may prosper, so that there will be no collecting when I come" (1 Cor. 16:2). It was already the "penny for the missions" of Pauline Jaricot. A committee, selected by the community, will be in charge of the fund (1 Cor. 6:3; 2 Cor. 8:23). To ensure transparency and keep clear of any suspicion of misappropriation, Paul will be accompanied by delegates from the churches to deliver the amount in Jerusalem (1 Cor. 16:4; Rom. 15:25).

These instructions followed similar practices of social solidarity in the Greco-Roman world. Synagogues as well as *collegia* had their mutual aid funds. The Diaspora showed its attachment to the Jerusalem Temple by generous contributions. As seen above, the royal court of Abiadene, for instance, had shown signaled generosity to the Temple and the city of Jerusalem. Disciples of Christ could not be less generous.

In the name of Christ, Paul asked them to be even more generous and to transcend the sociological limitations of clan, class, and ethnic belonging. Beyond the caritative aspect, the collection was part of his mission strategy. For Gentile Christians, it was a matter of identifying with the People of God, to be heirs of the promise made to Abraham.

> In his eyes, the collection was not merely a means of alleviating want; it was also recognition of Jerusalem's special status as the mother church of the new Israel, an acknowledgement on the part of the Gentile churches of their indebtedness to Jerusalem as the origin of spiritual blessings (Rom. 15:27), a demonstration to the Jerusalem church of the genuineness of the Gentile Christians' faith (2 Cor. 9:12f), and a bond of fellowship and love as a sign of unity between Jews and Gentiles in Christ.[17]

Prophets had announced that in the last days, all peoples, drawn to the glory of the Lord shining from Sion, would come bringing "the wealth of the nations."

---

17. R. Y. K. Fung, *The Epistle to the Galatians* (NICNT; Grand Rapids: Eerdmans, 1988), 102–3.

Nations shall come to your light, and kings to the brightness of your rising. Lift up your eyes all around, and see; they all gather together, they come to you; your sons shall come from afar, and your daughters shall be carried on the hip. Then you shall see and be radiant; your heart shall thrill and exult, because the abundance of the sea shall be turned to you, the wealth of the nations shall come to you. A multitude of camels shall cover you, the young camels of Midian and Ephah; all those from Sheba shall come. They shall bring gold and frankincense, and shall bring good news, the praises of the Lord. . . . For the coastlands shall hope for me, the ships of Tarshish first, to bring your children from afar, their silver and gold with them, for the name of the Lord your God, and for the Holy One of Israel, because he has made you beautiful. (Isa. 60:3–9)

Bringing to Jerusalem the fruit of the collection made among the Gentiles amounted to a pilgrimage to Sion to offer "the wealth of the nations."[18] The sharing of goods illustrated the emergence of the People of the New Covenant, gathering Jews and Gentiles in the common faith in Jesus Christ, the Risen One, the first fruits of the new creation. It carries the basic message of Paul's mission, expressed in deeds. As well as words, deeds proclaim the Word.

Letters as Communication Technique

The Word is relayed through letters. Speaking today of "communication" evokes modern techniques of instant audiovisual transmission. As the ancient world did not know these techniques, epistolary exchange was the communication system of the day. The Greco-Roman world made great use of it. A postal system had even been set up by Emperor Augustus. In staging posts, horses and horsemen could be replaced so that some eighty kilometers could be covered in a day. But this system was reserved to official mail and to military needs. Individuals depended on the good will of traveling friends and colleagues.

---

18. Cf. D. Lührmann *Galatians* (CC; Minneapolis: Fortress, 1992), 41.

To convey his letters, Paul could avail himself of the various networks of the Diaspora, of the professional corporations, and mostly of the solidarity of the local churches. Pauline letters make frequent reference to such journeys between communities; they provided opportunities to exchange mail. So Stephanas, Fortunatus, and Achaïcus had come from Corinth (1 Cor. 16:17). Apollos (1 Cor. 16:12) and Timothy (1 Cor. 16:10) had an opportunity to visit Corinth. Timothy had already been sent there to "remind of the ways in Christ" (1 Cor. 4:17). In fact, the entire 1 Corinthians is a response to a letter of the Corinthians asking for guidance on various points (1 Cor. 7:1). When Paul sent a letter through a messenger, the latter was also expected to explain its contents and, if needed, to dot the "i." For this kind of mission, Titus was not only a messenger but a mandated representative. In the crisis that affected the relationship between the Apostle and the Corinthians, he is entrusted with a severe letter (2 Cor. 7:8–12). He was able to present it in such a way that it released the tensions and had it accepted by the community (2 Cor. 7:6–7, 13–16). If, as widely held, chaps. 8 and 9 constituted one or two separate letters meant to promote the collection for the poor of Jerusalem, they would constitute the letter of authority giving mandate to Titus to handle the situation, as the head of the delegation entrusted with that mission.

Paul is a prolific writer. He may even have written more letters than those recorded in the canon. His writings are so deep that Renan could consider him as a "missed scholar."[19] Exegesis and theology will go on exploring the wealth of Pauline thought. But the function of the letters goes beyond their explicit contents. The correspondence itself has an underlying significance. The value of a letter does not depend only on the information that it conveys or the opinion that it expresses. The letter itself, or its absence, is a message by itself. A love letter, for instance, may have quite an insignificant content. Yet it carries a strong emotive load. Absence of correspondence, on the contrary, will

---

19. Quoted by M.-F. Baslez, *Saint Paul*, 336.

be alarming, by the very fact of its silence. What will be missed is not so much the absence of news as the form of substitutive presence that it conveys. It is so also for the letters sent by Paul to the churches. They are not theological treatises in disguise, "epistles" that would veil a philosophical or theological discourse. They are true letters addressed to specific groups in view of their particular problems.[20] They extend the presence of the Apostle who, through them, goes on participating in the life of the community. This function is bolstered by the personal tone of the letters. In the letter to the Galatians, for instance, the soberness of a midrashic argument is relieved by a moving reminder of the concern shown to the ailing Apostle (Gal. 4:13–16). The tone becomes affectionate when the missionary compares his attachment to that of a mother: "my little children, for whom I am again in the anguish of childbirth until Christ is formed in you!" (Gal. 4:19). And he concludes: "I wish I could be present with you now and change my tone, for I am perplexed with you" (Gal. 4:20). This conclusion is a perfect expression of what the letter signifies. It creates a virtual presence that tends to be as effective as a physical presence. Even the opponents have to recognize it: "His letters are weighty and strong" (2 Cor. 10:10).[21]

Another function of the letters is to connect the communities together and to foster the *koinōnia* of the *ekklēsiai*. The letters to the Romans, the Corinthians, and the Philippians end with lists of salutations. They are no mere polite greetings; they voice "love in

---

20. This applies as well to the letter to the Romans, in spite of its theological density. It is better realized now that the so called "theological" part (chaps. 2–8) is not the focal point of the letter. It only lays the ground to meet the concrete problem of the relationship between faithful coming from Judaism and those of the Gentiles (chaps. 9–11) and between "the strong" and "the weak" (chap. 14). The community must thus be solidly unified so that Paul may find in it a dependable basis for this drive toward the far west (chap. 15).

21. Cf. R. Bieringer, "Présence dans l'absence du corps," in *Paul's Graeco-Roman Context* (ed. C. Breytenbach; BETL 272; Leuven: Peeters, 2015), 357–74.

Christ Jesus" (1 Cor. 16:24). Those tiny groups scattered in the vast Mediterranean centers had to be reminded that they were part of a larger network united in the faith in Jesus Christ, the "first fruits" of the universal eschatological harvest (Rom. 16:5; 1 Cor. 16:15).

The churches were well aware of this powerful virtual presence. They kept the letters, copied them, and shared them. This form of respect toward the apostolic authority initiated what would become a canon in the likeness of the Scriptures of Israel.

Teamwork

Paul was no lonely worker. Acts as well as his letters shows him accompanied by one or several brothers. The heading of his letters associate him with a companion: Silvanus and Timothy (1 Thess. 1:1), Timothy alone (Phil. 1:1; 2 Cor. 1:1; Phlm. 1), Sosthenes (1 Cor. 1:1), anonymous "brothers" (Gal. 1:2). The only exception is the letter to the Romans, but it is not really an exception since there he has still to find partners in this Spanish venture. When we speak of the "epistles of St. Paul," we fail to do justice to those co-authors whom the Apostle associates explicitly with his message and his authority. In this association with a companion, he differs from itinerant philosophers who spread their personal ideology. This was not Paul's intention: the companion guaranteed that the message was that of a community.

The role of Timothy and Apollos and particularly of Titus has already been mentioned above. The detailed greetings that conclude Romans and 1 Corinthians reveal Paul's ability to mobilize cooperators. The couple of Aquila and Prisca was influential in fostering Paul's apostolate in Corinth; prominent members of the community (1 Cor. 16:19), they have been "fellow workers in Christ Jesus" (Rom. 16:3; cf. Acts 18:1–2, 26). Phoebe, a "deaconess,"[22] holds an important position: "she has been a patron of many" and of the Apostle himself. Paul does not

---

22. The Greek word *diakonos* is ambiguous. It would be an anachronism to give it a sacramental significance.

overlook the contribution of simple people. Urban is a "fellow worker in Christ" (v. 9); Mary "has worked hard" (v. 6) as well as Tryphaena and Tryphosa and "beloved Persis" (v. 12). The text does not specify what this collaboration and "hard work" involved. However this mixed picture evokes a community actively involved in the different aspects of the apostolic mission.

Among the collaborators, Barnabas deserves special mention. According to Acts, he is a leading figure of the church at its earliest beginning. This Levite from Cyprus is one of the first members of the Jerusalem community. He is presented as showing exemplary generosity in laying "at the feet of the apostles" the proceeds of the sale of his field (Acts 4:36–37). As an influential member of the community whose opinion is well heeded, he vouches for Saul, the young convert, whose sudden change of obedience is viewed with suspicion by the apostles (Acts 9:26–27). When the gospel reaches Antioch, he is delegated to ensure unity with the church of Jerusalem (Acts 11:22–24). One of his first initiatives is to draw Saul out of his confinement in Tarsus (Acts 9:3; 11:25). He is called by the Holy Spirit and by the Antiochian community to lead the first missionary campaign along with Paul (Acts 13:1–3). In this campaign, and, on common agreement, they will turn to the Gentiles (Acts 13:44–52). Therefore, they will go together to Jerusalem to defend this option (Acts 15:1–4).

Though less explicit, the epistles confirm the important role played by Barnabas in the first part of Paul's ministry. In 1 Corinthians 9:6, Paul and Barnabas have to meet the same criticism and make a joint defense of their policy to earn their livelihood. They go together to Jerusalem to advocate their Gentile option (Gal. 2:1) and consequently, it is to both of them that the "pillars" of the Jerusalem church extend "the right hand of fellowship" to seal the agreement that "we should turn to the Gentiles and they to the circumcision" (Gal. 2:9). The plural "we" is noteworthy. The Jerusalem Assembly does not address Paul individually but a solid team, strongly united by common labor and common trials, by a joint missionary option, well thought out in front of a strong opposition.

The break was all the more distressful. According to Acts, it was a superficial matter of disagreement about the capacity of Mark to rejoin the team (Acts 15:37–40). From Paul himself, we come to know that the disagreement was deeper. Barnabas sided with Peter on the occasion of the "Antiochian quarrel." The point at issue concerned the concessions made to Jewish Christians as regards meal regulations (Gal. 2:11–13). Paul was uncompromising: in Christ Jesus, there is no Jew and Greek (Gal. 3:28). We would like to know the other side of the debate and the reasons that prompted Barnabas to dissociate himself from Paul. Was it really "hypocrisy" on the part of Cephas? Did he not rather propose a compromise that would avoid a split? What was finally the issue of the argument? Did Paul manage to bring the community of Antioch to his side? He does not tell us how the quarrel ended. Carried by his spirited argument, he loses sight of his narrative and proceeds with his plea. Commentators generally agree that Paul did not win the day and that the community sided with Peter, supported by Barnabas.[23] Antioch will no longer be a base of apostolate for Paul, and there will be no letter to the Antiochians. Was Barnabas guilty of deception? Or, on the contrary, was not Paul too rigid? He was right, and the letter to the Galatians is a deep manifesto for freedom. But he may have been too much in the right. For him, the break was an unavoidable decision. For Barnabas, it must have been a wrenching issue. Paul was probably a strong character who knew how to lead a team of collaborators but found it difficult to become himself a collaborator.

---

23. Cf. Raymond E. Brown and John P. Meier, *Antioch and Rome* (London: Chapman, 1983), 39; S. Légasse, *L'épître de Paul aux Galates* (LDCom 9; Paris: Cerf, 2000), 165; L. Legrand, "The Antiochian Conflict in Gal 2:11–14," *VJTR* 83 (2019): 242–62.

10

To Another World: Inculturation

To announce the Good News, the Apostle faces a double challenge: he has to transpose the gospel message from Israel to the Gentiles and from its rural Galilean matrix to the urban cultural Greco-Roman milieu. He does it with creative boldness, inspired by the Spirit. Jesus announced the Good News to Galileans in the context of a remote province of the Roman Empire. Paul translated the message in the context and language of the Mediterranean world. By transplanting the gospel of the Galilean in the great centers of that world, Paul became the pioneer of inculturation.

Paul and Jesus

We have only to compare the style and methods of Jesus and of Paul to realize the creative originality of the Apostle to the Nations. Indeed, as regards mission practice, Paul does the opposite of the Galilean Messiah.

Apart from a few inroads in the territory of Tyre and Sidon, and in the Decapolis, the mission field of Jesus was limited to Palestine and even, if we go by the Synoptic Gospels, to the shores of the lake of Tiberias. The field of Paul extends to a major part of the Mediterranean basin.

Jesus's ministry was mainly rural: the "towns" of Galilee, mentioned in the Gospels, were quite small; they could not be compared with Thessalonica, Corinth, Athens, and Ephesus, not to speak of Rome. Within the restricted framework where he worked, Jesus seems to have avoided the main cities. He did not go to Sepphoris, the administrative capital of Roman Galilee, a few miles north of Nazareth. Neither did he preach in Tiberias, recently constructed by Herod Antipas in honor of Tiberius. Still less did he go to Caesarea, the seat of Roman power in Palestine. Pauline tactic, on the contrary, will target the main economic, political, and cultural centers of the empire.

The languages of Jesus and of Paul differed totally. Paul may not write in the Greek of professional writers; but his style is at least good, educated Greek. Reflecting the Aramaic spoken by Jesus, the Greek of the Gospels, but for Luke, remains basic. It is often parabolic, close to the life of poor rural people. The style of Paul is that of a man trained in Greek and Jewish patterns of thinking and writing.

Limited in space, the ministry of Jesus was also short in time. The Synoptics report only one Passover, the final one, and so they suggest a rapid and intense proclamation of the Good News. The chronology commonly accepted of a three years' ministry comes from the Gospel of John, which reports a triple Passover. As for the chronology of the Pauline ministry, if we put his vocation in 34–36 CE and the Roman captivity toward 60–62 CE, we get a duration of 25 years. Further, we can add the few years before his martyrdom, which is traditionally ascribed to 66–68 CE under Nero. The proclamation of the Good News by Jesus took the form of eschatological announcement. The preaching of Paul extended to the formation and on-going instruction of a network of *ekklēsiai*.

Limited in space and time, Jesus's mission ignores financial considerations. At night, missionaries will be received at home by sympathizers, and this will meet all their requirements (Mark 6:8–10 and par.). Paul's journeys are much longer; budgeting will be needed. From the small-scale textile industry run at home, he had learned to keep accounts. So, he will use the language of accountancy and speak with the Philippians of a "partnership in giving and receiving" (Phil. 4:15). Entering the spirit of the Mediterranean urban milieu, he will turn money into an instrument of apostolate. Through the collection organized in Greece in favor of the poor of Jerusalem (Rom. 15:25–28; 1 Cor. 16:1–4; 2 Cor. 8:9; Gal. 2:10), he will put Mammon at the service of Christian unity.

The following chart summarizes this contrast:

Jesus	*Paul*
Within Palestine, and mostly Galilee	Mediterranean world
Villager from Nazareth	Citizen of important town
Village "carpenter"[1]	Middle-class industrialist
Rural type of ministry	Urban type of ministry
Storyteller (parables)	Arguing style
From house to house (Mark 6:11)	From town to town
No human resources (Mark 6:8f)	Goes for financing (Phil. 4:15f; 2 Cor. 8f)

Consequently, should we take Paul as the antithesis of Jesus? Would he then be the inventor of a new religion, the founder of Christianity, as some have pretended? This would go counter to Paul's own witness: "I decided to know nothing among you except Jesus Christ and him crucified" (1 Cor. 2:2). It would also ignore the essential points on which Paul followed Jesus. For Paul as for Jesus, the essential message is the Good News of the fulfillment of the promises made to Israel. For both of them, Israel remains the stem of the People of God. But Israel, following the prophetical line, is called to enter into the new covenant according to the Spirit. This is the "foundation, which is Jesus

---

1. According to Mark 6:3, Jesus was a *tektōn* (the "son of a *tektōn*" according to Matt. 13:55). The Greek word may mean carpenter, wood worker, but also builder. In the restricted context of the small and poor village of Nazareth, there was no scope for full-time carpentry. In addition to woodwork, Jesus would have also helped to build and repair the humble houses of the village. He complemented the livelihood working as a farm hand during harvest time, grape and olive picking. Cf L. Legrand, *The Bible on Cultures* (New York: Orbis Books, 2004), 106–9.

Christ," other than which no one can lay another foundation (1 Cor. 3:11).

The difference between the Galilean Jesus and the Christ proclaimed by Paul comes from the fact that, due to the Resurrection, Paul finds himself called to make effective the universalism that could only remain virtual during the short span of time of Jesus's ministry. Now the message must resound "till the end of the earth" (Rom. 10:18; Ps. 19:5). Paul is the voice who proclaims this Word all over the earth, but the Word remains "the Word of Christ" (Rom. 10:17).

Paul and Hellenistic Philosophy

Paul's writings were influenced by Hellenistic rhetoric, but deeper was the influence of the philosophical currents of those days on his thought. The missionary from Tarsus could not escape the surrounding cultural atmosphere. Human being is a social being and shares with his contemporaries a way to look at society and at the world. Even if it is to oppose it, it is from within this common vision. Nowadays, for instance, the societal debate is no longer about feudalism but about the consuming society, social inequality, or ecology. However, we can hardly imagine Paul taking time to read and annotate the dialogues of Plato. Notwithstanding the authority of Jerome, we can remit to the apocrypha an exchange of letters between Paul and Seneca.[2] Yet one could not have been born and brought up in Tarsus, lived in Corinth, Ephesus, and Rome, without coming across Stoicism and its adepts. It was popularized by sophists who, from town to town, spread a "Philosophy for Dummies," which covered emptiness of thought under flowery language.[3] Paul could not but meet them.

---

2. Such apocryphal correspondence was composed in the fourth century CE and was widely spread in the Middle Ages. Cf. E. Hennecke, *New Testament Apocrypha* (London: Lutterworth, 1965), 2:133–41; P. Benoit, "Senèque et Saint Paul," in *Exégèse et théologie* (Paris: Cerf, 1961), 2:383–414; H. Leclercq, "Senèque et Paul," *DACL* 15, cols. 1193–98.

3. See J. C. Thom, "Paul and Popular Philosophy," in *Paul's Graeco-*

They are those whom he qualifies as "wise in a worldly way" (1 Cor. 3:18 NAB translation) and to whom he applies the words of Scripture: "He catches the wise in their craftiness," and again, "The Lord knows the thoughts of the wise, that they are futile" (1 Cor. 3:19–20). He has much more to offer than this vain "lofty speech of wisdom" (1 Cor. 2:1). Stoicism did not affect Paul's thought through bookish appropriation but through the influence of ideas floating in the collective mentality. He shares them, even when he has to correct them. For instance, when presenting celibacy as a condition that keeps one "free from anxieties" (*amerimnos*, 1 Cor. 7:32), "this text seems to be the passage in the Pauline epistles which comes closest to the stoic spirit; Paul seems to make his own the ideal of *ataraxia*, which the Stoic reaches by internal distancing from destiny."[4] When he exhorts "those who have wives to live as though they had none, and those who mourn as though they were not mourning, and those who rejoice as though they were not rejoicing, and those who buy as though they had no goods, and those who deal with the world as though they had no dealings with it" (1 Cor. 7:29–31), he is quite close to what Epictetus wrote more or less at the same time.[5] But Paul goes beyond Stoic autonomy. He adds immediately the specific Christian perspective of union with the Lord. If celibacy keeps one free from disquiet, it is "to secure undivided devotion to the Lord" (1 Cor. 7:36) and to be "anxious with the things of the Lord" (1 Cor. 7:32), in the same way as the Apostle carried the "anxiety for all the churches" (2 Cor. 11:27).

Roman Context (ed. C. Breytenbach; BETL 177; Leuven: Peeters, 2015), 47–74.

4. H. Conzelmann, *Der erste Brief an die Korinther* (KEK 5; Göttingen: Vandenhoeck & Ruprecht, 1969), 158.

5. "That you may not urge that I show you the example of a man clear of incumbrances, without a wife or children or country or friends or relations, to bend and draw him aside, take Socrates, and consider him, who had a wife and children, but held them not as his own; had a country, friends, relations, but held them only so long as it was proper, and in the manner that was proper" (Epictetus, *Discourses* 4.7).

Jesus had proclaimed the great command of love. He gave his life as an example of this love. But he had not gone into particulars. Paul had to translate the great command of love, to apply the "Law of the Spirit of life in Christ Jesus" (Rom. 8:2), to the larger framework of the Greco-Roman city and of the empire. When he declares, in Galatians 3:28, that "there is neither Jew nor Greek, neither slave nor free, no male and female," he extends the Christian horizon beyond the shores of the Sea of Galilee and opens the message of love to the dimensions of the Mediterranean world. Colossians 3:11 will go a step further by adding "barbarian and Scythian."

The influence of Stoicism was also relayed by Hellenistic Judaism, and it was under this influence that Paul could start formulating initial Christian ethics. The Jewish Diaspora had already enlarged the contents of the *Torah* to the dimension of the larger world. It had done so in dialogue with the leading trends of the days, particularly Stoicism. Paul draws inspiration from it.[6] He gives lists of virtues (2 Cor. 6:8–9; Phil. 4:8; Gal. 5:22–23) and of vices (Rom. 1:29–31; 13:13; 1 Cor. 5:10–11; 6:9–10; 2 Cor. 12:20–21; Gal. 5:19–21), which his followers will extend further (Col. 3:12; Eph. 4:2–3; 1 Tim. 4:12; 6:11; 2 Tim. 2:22; 3:10 for the virtues and Col. 3:5, 8; Eph. 5:3–5; 1 Tim. 1:9–10; 2 Tim. 3:2–5; Titus 3:3 for vices). These lists "are not of Paul's own making; they belong to a genre which, though absent in the Old Testament, are well represented in Hellenistic Judaism, for that matter indebted to popular Stoicism."[7]

Paul did not compose textbooks of Christian ethics or sociology. Rather, he initiated ethical reflection in response to the questions raised by life in community. We saw above his thoughts on marriage and celibacy. Women's liberation was clearly proclaimed in Galatians 3:28. Yet its application remained problematic in the running of Christian assemblies. The response was

---

6. For a detailed study, see C. Spicq, *Les épîtres pastorales* (EB; Paris: Gabalda,1969), 2:627–34.

7. S. Légasse, *L'épître de Paul aux Galates* (LDCom 9; Paris: Cerf, 2000), 423.

left to what common sense considered as "proper" (1 Cor. 11:13). After Paul, his successors will work out well-defined household codes (Eph. 5:22–6:9; Col. 3:18–4:1; Tit. 2:1–10; 1 Pet. 2:13–3:7). On the basis of Paul's teaching and rooted in Jesus's Torah of love, Christian ethics continued to grow in response to emerging life problems and in dialogue with cultural trends and thought currents of the times.

Paul and the Leading Concepts of Greek Culture

Socially recognized values function as driving forces under the lifestyles and patterns of thought that characterize societies. We think for instance of the mobilizing force of the ideas of *Swatantra* and *Satyagraha* in the struggle for the independence of India. We cannot here go into an analysis of what constituted the heart of Greek culture. We can, however, follow Paul himself when he identifies three leading themes that stirred people's mind in his days: wisdom, freedom, and glory.

Wisdom

Paul's diagnosis is clear and accurate: "Greeks seek wisdom" (1 Cor. 1:22). He knew that he did not miss the mark when praising Corinthians for "being enriched in all speech and knowledge" (1 Cor. 1:5). "Knowledge" (*gnōsis*) was later to take a religious turn in the Gnostic movements that will claim initiatory access to deeper mysteries. But, for Paul, this "knowledge" and this "wisdom" must stand the test of "the folly of the Cross" and of the "mind of Christ" (1 Cor. 2:16).

"The mind of Christ" is the true wisdom. "For Paul, Christ refers regularly to the Crucified One (1 Cor. 1:17, 23f, 30; 2:2; 15:3; Rom. 5:6, 8; 6:3, 8, etc.), and the Apostle means this: the mind of God, the secret of his purpose cannot be known unless one has *the mind of* Christ, faith that recognizes true wisdom in the folly of the 'word of the cross.'"[8] Paul and his addressees share in the

---

8. C. Senft, *La première épître de Saint Paul aux Corinthiens* (CNT 7; Geneva: Labor et Fides, 1990), 54.

same mental horizon as the surrounding cultural world; they give absolute value to knowledge and wisdom. But facing "the depth of the riches and wisdom and knowledge of God" (Rom. 11:33), the wisdom of the world appears to be folly. "The wisdom of this world is folly with God. For it is written, 'He catches the wise in their craftiness,' and again, 'The Lord knows the thoughts of the wise, that they are futile'" (1 Cor. 3:19–20). God's wisdom is manifested in the folly of love shown on the cross. The "language of the Cross" puts to naught the wisdom of the wise and the cleverness of the clever. "For it is written, 'I will destroy the wisdom of the wise, and the discernment of the discerning I will thwart.' Where is the one who is wise? Where is the scribe? Where is the debater of this age? Has not God made foolish the wisdom of the world?" (1 Cor. 1:19–20). It is the Cross that leads to "the surpassing worth of knowing Christ Jesus my Lord. . . . that I may know him and the power of his Resurrection, and may share his sufferings, becoming like him in his death" (Phil. 3:8–10).

The conclusion remains within the ambit of wisdom but of converted wisdom:

> Among the mature we do impart wisdom, although it is not a wisdom of this age or of the rulers of this age. . . . But we impart a secret and hidden wisdom of God, which God decreed before the ages for our glory. . . . These things God has revealed to us through the Spirit. . . . Now we have received not the spirit of the world, but the Spirit who is from God, that we might understand the things freely given us by God. And we impart this in words not taught by human wisdom but taught by the Spirit. (1 Cor. 2:6–13)

An heir to Paul, well versed in the mind of his master, described in deep terms this knowledge given by the Spirit:

> [May the Father] grant you to be strengthened with power through his Spirit in your inner being, so that Christ may dwell in your hearts through faith, that you, being rooted and grounded in love, may have strength to comprehend

with all the saints what is the breadth and length and height and depth, and to know the love of Christ that surpasses knowledge, that you may be filled with all the fullness of God. (Eph. 3:16–19)

"To know the love of Christ that surpasses knowledge": this is the true *gnosis*, and the true wisdom, converted into "language of the Cross" and transformed by the power of his Resurrection.

Freedom

Freedom is another leading concept of the Greek world. To defend their freedom against Persian aggression, Greeks had fought victoriously at Marathon, Salamis, and Plataea. Aeschylus had staged this glorious combat in a popular tragedy, *The Persians*. In the Hellenic imagination, this battle of Greek democracy against the tyranny of the "great kings," Darius and Xerxes, was the equivalent of the Statue of Liberty at the entrance of New York harbor. The situation had changed since Athens and Macedonia had lost their preeminence to Alexandria and Antioch finally to end under Roman domination. Rome itself had swung from republic to empire. Yet liberty was still considered as the supreme good, at least for the free citizens. "Freedom is the greatest good and slavery is the most miserable condition," said a Latin proverb.[9] Epictetus, who himself had been a slave, interiorized the concept of liberty by showing how even a slave can be free. "The Stoic is the slave who sets himself free by negating the master and, with him, any external attachment. At the same time, he reveals to the master the secret of true freedom, which consists in dominating not the slave but himself."[10] This is what Epictetus explains at the beginning of his *Discourses:*

What says Zeus? "Epictetus, if it were possible, I would have made your little body . . . free and not exposed to hindrance. . . . Since I was not able to do for you what I have mentioned,

---

9. Quoted by Dio Chrysostom, *Or* 14.1.
10. E. Bréhier, *Les Stoïciens* (La Pléiade; Paris: Gallimard, 1962), 806.

I have given you a small portion of us, this faculty of pursuing an object and avoiding it, and the faculty to will and not to will. . . . If you will take care of this faculty and consider it your only possession, you will never be hindered, never meet with impediments; you will not lament, you will not blame, you will note flatter any person."[11]

Freedom, however, is not an Old Testament theme. It is true that liberation from the yoke of the Pharaoh and the end of the Babylonian captivity are foundational events of Israel's faith in a Savior God. But paradoxically it is not the words "freedom" and "liberation" that express this faith. The Hebrew words *hophshi* (free) and *hophshit* (freedom) are rarely used and only in the concrete case of freed slaves. N. Lohfink notes the absence of *hophshit* in the soteriological Old Testament language and that in spite of the importance of Exodus as liberation from Egypt. He concludes: "On the one hand, the theology of Exodus will lead to the abrogation of human slavery but, on the other hand, it will not result in a theology of freedom but in a theology of subjection to God."[12]

It follows that Paul uses a Greek and not a biblical language when he describes the Christian condition as a situation of freedom. In Galatians 4:21–31, he spoke as a Jewish rabbi in the intricate midrash on the two wives of Abraham. Yet, in conclusion, he takes another tone and speaks as a citizen of the Hellenistic world when he proclaims high and loud: "For freedom Christ has set us free; stand firm therefore, and do not submit again to a yoke of slavery. . . . You were called to freedom, brothers" (Gal. 5:1, 13). Freedom is the condition of the Christians. They have received the Spirit of Christ and "where the Spirit of the Lord is, there is freedom" (2 Cor. 3:17).

---

11. *Discourses* 1.1.10–12. The first part of *Discourses* Book 4 is devoted to the analysis of true freedom (4.1–177). Diogenes and Socrates are given as models (151–69).

12. N. Lohfink, art. *hophshit, TDOT* 5:117–18.

But Paul adds immediately: "Only do not use your freedom as an opportunity for the flesh, but through love serve one another, for the whole Law is fulfilled in one word: 'You shall love your neighbor as yourself'" (Gal. 5:13–14). There lies the difference between Christian and Stoic freedom: the latter consists in being liberated from any attachment so as to reach a state of absolute quiet peace of mind (*ataraxia*).[13] For Paul, on the contrary, liberty consists in self-surrender prompted by love. He does not hesitate to use the word "enslavement" to express this oblative love. Under the impulsion of the Spirit, the "flesh" is "crucified" (Gal. 5:24–25) and the Spirit can yield his fruits, "love, joy, peace, patience, kindness" (Gal. 5:22).

Paul speaks to Greeks in their language: he speaks of freedom. But he lays freedom at the foot of the cross where it takes its genuine meaning, not of self-sufficiency, but of self-surrender out of love in the power of the Spirit. There is no freedom but in love.

Glory

The theme of glory presents the interest of being bi-cultural. It is Greco-Roman as well as biblical. From Rome to North Africa, passing through Gaul and Spain, the Mediterranean world was filled with triumphal arches "to the glory" of emperors, conquerors, and generals. Athletes in the stadium, poets and philosophers on the agora or on the forum also claimed glory and fame. So did patricians and enriched businessmen, parading round the capitol surrounded by their clients. Wealth itself was subordinated to glory: it could serve to finance circus games and gladiators' fights to the glory of the sponsor.

---

13. "When somebody has this peace, not from Caesar—for how should he be able to proclaim it?—but by God through his word (*logos*), is he not content when he is alone? He sees and reflects. Now no evil can happen to me; for me there is no robber, no earthquake, everything is full of peace, full of tranquility (*ataraxia*)" (Epictetus, *Discourses* 3.13.12–13).

The Bible also speaks of glory: the glory of Abraham (Gen. 13:2), of Joseph in Egypt (Gen. 45:13), of Solomon (1 Kgs. 3:13), the glory of the splendor of the Temple (Hag. 2:3, 7, 9), of Jerusalem (Isa. 62:2). But mostly, glory belongs to God. It is manifested in the Sinai theophanies (Exod. 24:15–18; Deut. 5:22–26), on the occasion of the consecration of the Temple (1 Kgs. 8:10–12) or in the visions granted to the prophets (Isa. 6:1–5; Ezek. 1:1–28). It leaves sinful Jerusalem as a punishment (Ezek. 10:1–2), but it will return when the people will have been forgiven, purified, and revived (Ezek. 43:4–7). It is this glory that will attract the nations to the splendor of a transfigured Jerusalem (Isa. 60:1–7).

For Rome and Athens, as well as for Jerusalem, glory is an ultimate value. But they give a different meaning to the word. In Greek, the glory is *doxa*, a word that originally meant opinion, fame, renown, celebrity, which implies that glory or honor comes from the way one is considered by others. There is no glory or fame in solitude. Glory depends on looks from outside, marked by admiration or scorn, uplifting or lowering in the social scale, giving power or debasing. In Hebrew, glory is *kabod*, from a root that means weight (*kabed*). Having glory means being weighty. The word connotes inner value. Abraham was "weighty" by the richness of his flock and of his wealth (Gen. 13:2). Joseph exercised a "weighty" influence at the court of the Pharaoh (Gen. 45:13). The glory of the Temple came from its divine irradiation (Hag. 2:3, 7). Biblical glory is not the reflection of an external outlook; it is the expression of an internal force. This applies primarily to God. Psalms and hymns sing the glory of God, but his glory does not depend on praise from outside. Glory emanates from within the divine entity. Glory belongs to God for all eternity (Gal. 1:5). God is perceived as a fiery focus of unbearable light. It irradiates with such intensity that one cannot see it and live (cf. Isa. 6:4), come into contact with it and survive (2 Sam. 6:6–8). It was a way to express the transcendent holiness of the Most High, his "majesty, power, the brightness of his holiness, the dynamism of his being."[14] The glory of God is his "majesty,

14. Cf. D. Mollat, art. "Glory," *DBT*, 202–3.

dominion, and authority before all time and now and forever" (Jude 25; cf. Rom. 11:36; 16:27; Gal. 1:5; Eph. 3:21; 1 Tim. 1:17; 2 Tim. 4:18).

This glory was manifested in the theophanies, but the ultimate theophany was "the glory that shines on the face of Christ" (2 Cor. 4:6), revealed to Paul on the way to Damascus. It shines in "the light of the gospel of the glory of Christ, who is the image of God" (2 Cor. 4:5). It irradiates the ministry of the new covenant in the Spirit: "And all of us, with our unveiled faces like mirrors reflecting the glory of the Lord, are being transformed into the image that we reflect in brighter and brighter glory; this is the working of the Lord who is the Spirit" (2 Cor. 3:18).[15]

The glory of God manifested on the face of the Crucified and Risen One, transmitted by the Good News and entrusted to its ministers: such is the meaning of apostolate, and it carries a weight of glory far superior to the superficial glory sought by the world. The contrast between the glory of God and human glory is so strong that, for Paul, the latter does not deserve to be called "glory." To God only belongs glory. Human glory can only be called "boasting," "taking pride."[16] In the sociocultural context of those days, this human boasting is no mere showing off. It is the attitude that intends to intimidate others and browbeat them through pretended superiority. It is the ego projecting its crushing presence in society. It belongs to a value system that is the absolute opposite of "the face of Christ," haloed with the glory of self-surrender on the cross. This diametrical contrast of the two value systems is well summarized in the words of Jesus:

> Those who are considered rulers of the Gentiles lord it over them, and their great ones exercise authority over them. But it shall not be so among you. But whoever would be great among you must be your servant, and whoever would be

---

15. Translation of the *NJB*.

16. It is expressed by the Greek verb *kauchasthai*, which occurs 35 times. The noun *kauchēsis*, action of taking pride, occurs 10 times and *kauchēma*, the object of pride 10 times. For Paul, the only *kauchēma* is the Cross.

first among you must be slave of all. For even the Son of
Man came not to be served but to serve, and to give his life
as a ransom for many. (Mark 10:42–45)

To those who boast and lord it over others, Paul responds by
irony. He borrows their language but in a subversive manner,
reversing its meaning. He boasts but of his weakness (2 Cor.
11:23–35); he takes pride, but in his humiliations, (2 Cor. 12:1–10).
He is in line with the Beatitudes: Joy for the poor! Power to the
weak! He was not there on the mountain, sitting at the feet of the
Master. But he met the Risen One whom he knew to have under-
gone the disgracing execution on the cross. There he received the
revelation of true glory, the glory of One who took the form of
a slave tortured unto death but whom God exalted above every
name (Phil. 2:8–9). Following Jesus, Paul stands for a counterculture. However, it should be noted that this counterculture does
not mean evading to another world. Paul does not lead the believers to the weird imaginations of apocalypticism. It is from within
the system that he challenges its values and overturns them.

The dominating culture of the Greco-Roman world gave privileged value to a glory that flaunted the ego and subjugated the
other. The gospel culture will promote servanthood to the other
(Phil. 2:4), in the image of the Servant. The song of love in 1 Corinthians 13 will be the hymn of this new culture.

Conclusion

Between Paul and Jesus, the union of hearts is deep, but the cultural distance is vast. It was the task of Paul's genial boldness to
transpose the Good News of Jesus the Galilean to the cultural
context of the Mediterranean world. This transposition had different aspects. Concerning freedom, Paul borrows the theme
itself from Greek culture and thereby Christian language was
enriched by the wealth of Greek history and thought. To some
extent, a similar enrichment came from the encounter with the
kind of popular Stoicism that pervaded Greco-Roman mentality.

On the opposite, concerning wisdom and glory, the Apostle

lays more emphasis on the contrast between wisdom and folly, self-assertion, and enslavement. His is the subversive language of counterculture. However, this criticism does not stem from the intrusion of a foreign culture. The "scandal of the Cross" addresses the very heart of the quest for wisdom that torments the Greeks.

Anyway, whether it be in a spirit of dialogue or of challenge, the ultimate criterion of Christian language remains the "language of the Cross" (1 Cor. 1:18). In front of the harsh reality of the Cross, the encounter of the gospel with cultures cannot melt into debilitating assimilation. The Cross remains a "scandal to the Jews and folly to the Greeks" (1 Cor. 1:23). Paul has denounced the universal sway of sin: "all have sinned; all fall short of the glory of God" (Rom. 3:23; cf. 5:12–21). He can as well denounce the weight of sin carried by any human culture, whether pagan (Rom. 1:18–32) or Jewish (Rom. 2:1–15).

The encounter between gospel and culture is to take place in depth and in many different manners: this is what the example of Paul shows. "Inculturation" does not consist only in covering rites and cult with a superficial varnish. It must penetrate the deep-seated level of the ways of thinking, speaking, and situating oneself in society and in the world. It will reach the substratum of thought and action that governs individual and social life, the conscious and unconscious value system that determines judgments and priorities. Such were the new dimensions that Paul brought to the message of the Galilean.

Is the term "inculturation" an adequate expression of what the Apostle lived and did? The term "inculturation" carries overtones of intrusion. The suffix "-ation" suggests a deliberate intervention of an agent on the subject. Paul did not "practice" inculturation in a deliberate and artificial manner. He just lived his faith in the Risen One in his Judeo-Hellenistic being in solidarity with the world of the nations which he adopted as his own. He belonged to this world, and it was from within this belonging that he lived and expressed his faith in a new language. He did it with boldness and originality but not as a foreigner intruding from outside.

We could better speak of emergence. The new language of Christian faith which the Apostle created emerged from his immersion in a world crisscrossed by intertwined cultural currents.

Paul has been indeed the Apostle to the Nations. He was so not only by the extent of the territory that he covered but, more deeply, because he gave Christian faith the equipment that enabled it to enter the plurality of peoples and of their cultures.

PART THREE

The Power at Work in the Mission

The Apostle goes from Syrian Antioch to Pisidian Antioch, from Asia Minor to Illyria and on to Rome as a base of a drive to Spain, to the western extremity of the earth, in the midst of oppositions, misunderstandings, scourging, and death threats. We cannot but be stunned by such an amazing energy. He seems to be driven by a superhuman force, exceeding human capacities. What is that force that sustained him? How did he draw from this force?

11

The Power of His Resurrection

Facing the awesome task entrusted to him, the Apostle is aware of his weakness. He often refers to it. Where is he going to draw the force that impels him when he would have good reasons to feel discouraged? What is the power that inhabits his weakness?

The Power of the Spirit

In the Acts of the Apostles, Luke considers the Holy Spirit as "the protagonist of the mission,"[1] and especially of the Pauline mission. It is the Holy Spirit that, during a liturgical gathering of the church in Antioch, takes the initiative to send Paul and Barnabas "for the work to which I have sent them" (Acts 13:1–3). This is an important moment. The text serves as a prologue to the part of the book that will be devoted to the mission of Paul: the entire action of the Apostle is placed under the guidance and the power of the Spirit. The Spirit gives force to the words and deeds of the messengers (Acts 13:9; 19:6). The Spirit stirs the communities and fills them with joy as they listen to the Word (Acts 13:52). On the occasion of the great debate of Jerusalem, it is again the Spirit that cautions with authority the major options of the mission to the Gentiles (Acts 15:8–9, 28). Occasionally, the Spirit will even alter the apostolic planning.

---

1. In the terms of the encyclical of John Paul II on *The Mission of Christ the Redeemer*, III, 21.

When Paul and Silas intend to resume the course followed in the first journey, the Spirit thwarts their project, "forbids them" to go around in circles again, and pushes them farther west toward the ends of the earth, toward Troas, at the far end of Asia (Acts 16:6–9) where the vision of a Macedonian will make them cross over to Greece, to Europe. At the end of the book, the "word of the Spirit" in the Scriptures will be the final pronouncement that concludes the whole story: "salvation of God for all nations" (Acts 28:25–28).

This viewpoint corresponds to the theology of Luke in Acts. He had put the gift of the Spirit as a heading to the entire story in Acts 1:8 and had illustrated it by the programmatic description of the work of the Spirit on Pentecost day in Acts 2:1–13. At a deeper level, this work was rooted in the coming of the Spirit on Mary to conceive and bear the Son of God, at the origin and as the font of the divine design (Luke 1:35).

In so doing, Luke presented the gospel proclamation as the fulfillment of a fundamental biblical theme. In the Old Testament, it was the Spirit that stirred the judges of Israel (Judges 3:10; 6:34; 11:29; 14:6; 1 Sam. 11:6), anointed the kings with authority (1 Sam. 10:11; 16:13), and inspired the prophets (Exod. 15:20; 1 Sam. 10:6; 1 Kgs. 18:20; Ezek. 2:2; 3:12, 24; 8:3; 11:5). Finally, it was the Spirit who consecrated the Messiah, royal (Isa. 11:2) as well as prophetical (Isa. 61:1–2).

> The Spirit of the Lord God is upon me, because the Lord has anointed me to bring good news to the poor; he has sent me to bind up the broken hearted, to proclaim liberty to the captives, and the opening of the prison to those who are bound; to proclaim the year of the Lord's favor, and the day of vengeance of our God; to comfort all who mourn. (Isa. 61:1–2)

In the Gospel of Luke, Jesus quotes this text as the prologue and main guideline of his messianic mission. The apostolic mission in Acts follows the same leadership of the Spirit.

"The Spirit Who Raised Jesus from the Dead"

Before Luke already, Paul made frequent reference to the power of the Spirit. Summarizing his ministry in the letter to the Romans, he describes it as the work of the Spirit: "I will not venture to speak of anything except what Christ has accomplished through me to bring the Gentiles to obedience, by word and deed, by the power of signs and wonders, by the power of the Spirit of God, . . . I have fulfilled the ministry of the gospel of Christ" (Rom. 15:18–19). He had described his Macedonian ministry in similar terms. "Our gospel came to you not only in word, but also in power and in the Holy Spirit and with full conviction" (1 Thess. 1:5). The power of the Spirit gives power and potency to a language deprived of any human attractiveness. "I was with you in weakness and in fear and much trembling, and my speech and my message were not in plausible words of wisdom, but in demonstration of the Spirit and of power, that your faith might not rest in the wisdom of men but in the power of God" (1 Cor. 2:3–5). The same power of the Spirit is also at work in the believers' community by multiplying its gifts in it. He has to remind the Galatians of this work of the Spirit among them: "Having begun by the Spirit, are you now being perfected by the flesh? Did you suffer so many things in vain, if indeed it was in vain? Does he who supplies the Spirit to you and works miracles among you do so by works of the Law, or by hearing with faith? (Gal. 3:3–5). Corinthians who boasted of the profusion of their charisms are reminded that they are gifts of the Spirit "for the common good" (1 Cor. 12:7) and that the Spirit is the principle of unity of the same body, the body of Christ (1 Cor. 12:13).

Now, for Paul, the Spirit is not a vague power floating in the air as a kind of ectoplasm. The Spirit is narrowly connected with the person of Christ. To perceive the mind of Paul, we must now return to his encounter with the risen Christ. Saul the scribe saw it as the fulfillment of Ezekiel's prophecy announcing the resurrection of Israel's dry bones by the power of the Spirit (Ezek. 37:9–14). The Spirit is essentially "the Spirit of him who raised

Jesus from the dead" (Rom. 8:11), "the Spirit of Christ" (Rom. 8:9), "the Spirit of life in Christ Jesus" (Rom. 8:2). The Good News concerning the Son of God consists in proclaiming that the One "who descended from David according to the flesh" has been "constituted Son of God in power according to the Spirit of holiness by his Resurrection from the dead" (Rom. 1:3–4). For Paul, the Spirit is perceived through the Risen One.

He can even say, "The Lord is the Spirit" (2 Cor. 3:17–18). From patristic times onward, flows of commentaries have been written on this statement, obscure in its concision. It should not be taken as a dogmatic statement confusing the persons of the Trinity. It is not a matter of ontological identity but of role in the work of salvation. In the context of 2 Corinthians 3, we understand that, in the "Lord," the Risen Christ, whatever has been said above about the Spirit finds its fulfillment in the Alliance according to the vivifying Spirit (2 Cor. 3:6), the freedom according to the Spirit (v. 7), the source of the "ministry of the Spirit" (v. 8). The creative and liberating action of the Spirit is actualized in the person of the Risen Christ.

As in Luke and before him, the power at work in the Apostle is the power of the Spirit. But, unlike in Acts, this power of the Spirit finds a concrete expression in the Risen Lord. For Paul, Christology and pneumatology are intertwined. Paul perceives the Spirit through the Risen One and the Risen One as the One who carries the power of the Spirit.

"The Power of His Resurrection"

The power of the Spirit embodied in the Resurrection of Christ is forcefully summarized in Philippians 3:9–10. Evoking the episode of his vocation, Paul recalls the revelation of "the surpassing worth of knowing Christ Jesus the Lord" (Phil. 3:8). It will be the soul of his life and of his action: "that I may gain Christ and be found in him, . . . that I may know him and the power of his Resurrection, and may share his sufferings, becoming like him in his death" (Phil. 3:8–10). In this terse statement, every word should be pondered:

- "Know": in the biblical sense of the word. It does not connote only abstract knowledge; it implies communion and commitment. Paralleling the "communion in the sufferings of Christ" referred to in the second part of the sentence, this "knowledge" carries the same connotations of intimate sharing, of fusion of heart.
- "Know *him*": the "surpassing worth," the supreme good is the heart to heart union with Jesus Christ. The believer who knows *him* can say: "we have the mind of Christ" (1 Cor. 2:16). The power of the Spirit does not work in a disincarnated manner; it acts in and through the humanity of Jesus. The Spirit exercises the power of the Resurrection in the humanity of Jesus and the fusion of hearts takes place with a human being: "To me, to live is Christ" (Phil. 1:21). This is not Gnosticism or Platonism. It is the logic of Incarnation.
- "The power of his Resurrection": it is the power of the Spirit who raised Jesus from the dead" and thereby established "the new covenant," and initiated the "new creation" (2 Cor. 5:17; Gal. 6:15).
- "That I may share his sufferings": saying "to me to live is Christ" entails as a consequence "to die is gain." It is the other side of the "knowledge" and "communion" in which is fully realized the logic of Incarnation. The Cross brings down to earth firmly the work of the Spirit and the power of the Resurrection. They do not operate in an Edenic world or an ethereal heaven but in the realities of life and death, which Paul qualifies as the "flesh," that is, in the human condition marked with frailty and ambiguity. The Cross means that God sent his Son "in the likeness of sinful flesh" (Rom. 8:3) and that the Son shared in the human distresses, unto death, so that they may give access to the power of a new life in the Spirit.

  The logic of the Incarnation is the logic of the Cross. This is what Paul called the "the language of the Cross, folly to those who are perishing, . . . but to those who are called, both Jews and Greeks, Christ the power of God and the wisdom of God" (1 Cor. 1:18, 24). Paul speaks in identical terms of the power of the Cross and of the power of the Resurrection. They are the two faces of the same mystery. The Risen One is the Crucified One who assumed fully the human condition, the one who knew no sin and that God "made to be sin" (2 Cor. 5:21). Reciprocally, the Crucified One is the Risen One, in whom is manifested the power of the life-giving Spirit.

• "Becoming like him in his death": the Greek word is *symmorphos*. The prefix *sym-* connotes communion. The root *morph-* recalls the similar occurrence in the christological hymn of the previous chapter: He who was in *morphē* of God "made himself nothing, taking the *morphē* of a servant" (Phil. 2:7). Sharing in the *morphē* of Christ implies entering the mystery of self-emptying, of kenosis, which took the Son of God to the Cross. As a commentator on Philippians has written,

> Sharing in the sufferings of Christ is specified here as an identification of Paul's way with the one described in Phil. 2:6–8. . . . Jesus spurned the honors to which he was entitled by his equality with God and Paul renounced his privileges, in a radical way since he suffered the loss of all things and counted them as rubbish. Jesus wanted to be in everything like unto men, and Paul turned toward the Lord to identify with him. Finally, as Christ went to death on the cross, the apostle shares in his sufferings and becomes like him in his death.[2]

"Knowing the power of his Resurrection" implies communion with the radical love that leads to the Cross. Cross and Resurrection are the two indissociable aspects of what Jesus Christ signifies. They hinge on the Cross. The Cross reveals the transcendent intensity of this love; Resurrection reveals its power. There lies the heart of the Pauline mission, the Spirit of the mission; the life and work of the Apostle are impelled by the love that Christ showed in his death on the cross.

---

2. J.-N. Aletti, *Saint Paul: Épître aux Philippiens* (EB 55; Paris: Gabalda, 2005), 250.

In another text, Paul expresses powerfully how he has been grasped by the love of Christ. "The love of Christ has a hold on us as we realize that one has died for all and therefore all have died" (2 Cor. 5:14).[3] This text is often quoted as an expression of apostolic zeal. The meaning would be that Paul's love for Christ urges him to dedicate himself totally to his mission and stirs him to face all ordeals.[4] This rendering misses the essential point. As shown in the parallel text of Romans 8:31–39, "the love of Christ" is the "love of God in Christ Jesus our Lord," the love that God has for us, he "who did not spare his own son but gave him up for us all" (v. 31). This love which is proper to God has been "poured into our hearts through the Holy Spirit who has been given to us" (Rom. 5:5). When Paul speaks of "the love of Christ which has taken hold of us," he does not refer to human generosity, even uplifted by grace, but to the almighty power of the divine love, infinitely superior to any power (Rom. 8:37–39).

Another exclamation of Paul must be understood in the same spirit: "Woe to me if I do not preach the gospel" (1 Cor. 9:16). The context explains why he prided himself on asking nothing from the Corinthians. He could have demanded being provided with the means for his upkeep. The Lord himself had authorized him (v. 14) as well as the Law (vv. 7–10). Such was also the practice of the priests in the Temple (v. 13). If he had run his own business, he could have expected some gain. But he was only fulfilling the mandate he had received. He qualifies this mandate as "a necessity laid upon" him. The Greek word is strong: *anankē* is fate, the unescapable destiny, a divinized principle that commands one's life. Paul cannot understand

---

3. Translators render in different ways the Greek verb *synechei*: "control" (RSV, ESV), "impel" (NAB, NLT), "compel" (NIV). The verb evokes a force that takes possession like the fever that "took possession" of Peter's mother-in-law (Luke 4:38) or the fear that takes hold of the witnesses of an exorcism (Luke 8:37). In any case, "the love of Christ" is not the love which Paul has for Christ but the love that Jesus has for us.

4. As implied in the NRSV translation: "the love of Christ urges us on."

it as a blind, tyrannical destiny; it is rather the divine plan of salvation, the collaborator of which he has been invited to be. This vocation works like a "divine constraint which he cannot brush away"[5] But this constraint is not an alienating external force. Paul has assumed and interiorized it. His words "echo the words of Jeremiah constrained to proclaim the word of God (Jer. 1:6–7; 20:9)":[6] "If I say, 'I will not mention him, or speak any more in his name,' there is in my heart as it were a burning fire shut up in my bones, and I am weary with holding it in, and I cannot" (Jer. 20:9; cf. Amos 3:8). Paul's mission has become the exclusive contents of his thought and action."[7] It is an overwhelming weight and a burning fire, but it has also become an integral part of his existence. When Paul says, "woe to me if I do not preach the gospel," he does not refer to a condemnation that would come from outside, a sanction imposed on an attitude of disobedience.[8] He speaks rather of the internal distress felt by one who lives in contradiction with his deepest impulses. The "necessity" laid upon him does not come from a yoke imposed from outside but from the deep-seated thrust of his existence. Paul has experienced "the power of his Resurrection," and it is that power that drives his life and action.

In the same vein, he says: "Christ Jesus took hold of me" (Phil. 3:12),[9] or, more radically: "It is no longer I who live, but Christ who lives in me" (Gal. 2:20). He could say as well: "It is no longer I who am at work, but Christ works in me." This is indeed what he says: "I will not venture to speak of anything except what Christ has accomplished through me to bring the Gentiles to obe-

---

5. W. Grundmann, art. *anankē, TDNT,* 1:346.

6. J. A. Fitzmyer, *First Corinthians* (AB 32; New Haven: Yale University Press, 2009), 367.

7. A. Strobel, art. *anankē, EDNT* 1:79.

8. "The *ouai* is not a threat of punishment but the constatation of one's sad situation" (M. Quesnel, *La première épître aux Corinthiens* [CBNT 7; Paris: Cerf, 2018], 223).

9. NJB translation and also NIV and NEV.

dience, by word and deed, by the power of signs and wonders, by the power of the Spirit of God" (Rom. 15:18–19).

The deep fountain head at the heart of apostolic action is more than an ardent zeal that would be sustained by the Spirit. It is the Spirit of the Risen One himself which instills in the mission all the power of the divine love.

12

The Apostle in Prayer

Since the mission rests on the power of the Spirit manifested in Jesus's Resurrection, the Apostle who has been entrusted with this mission will remain connected with this power through prayer. So was Paul, "a man of prayer."[1] Remaining within the framework of this study, we shall focus on the way in which, according to the Apostle, mission and prayer are interconnected.

Frequency

Prayer takes an important place in the Pauline letters. With the lone exception of Galatians, all the letters of the Apostle begin with a prayer and conclude with a blessing. In the course of the letter, a prayer will often break the course of the exposition, or rather animate and reorient it. In addition to elaborate prayers, short invocations are scattered through the epistles. Prayer can

---

1. According to the title of the book of C. Tassin, *Paul, homme de prière* (Paris: Éditions de l'Atelier, 2003); cf. P. Schubert, *Form and Function of Pauline Thanksgiving* (BZNW 20; Berlin: Töpelmann, 1939); G. Delling, *Worship in the New Testament* (London: Darton, Longman & Todd, 1962); J. T. Sanders, *The New Testament Christological Hymns* (SNTSMS 15; Cambridge: Cambridge University Press, 1971); G. P. Wiles, *Paul's Intercessory Prayers* (SNTSMS 24, Cambridge: Cambridge University Press, 1974); P. T. O'Brien, *Introductory Thanksgivings in the Letters of Paul* (SNT 49; Leiden: Brill, 1977); J. Thuruthumaly, *Blessing in St Paul* (Alwaye: Pontifical Institute Publications, 1981); Tony Costa, *Worship and the Risen Jesus in the Pauline Letters* (SBLit 157; New York: Peter Lang, 2013).

express joyful thanksgiving (Rom. 7:25; 1 Cor. 15:57; 2 Cor. 9:15), intercession (1 Thess. 3:11–13; 5:23), take a hymnic form (Rom. 8:31–37; 11:33–36; Phil. 2:6–11; 4:20), or express a blessing (Rom. 15:33). These short prayers are, so to say, the breathing of the text. It is in a spirit of prayer that Paul writes his letters and keeps contact with his communities.

This integration of prayer in letters was no common feature of ancient letters. It hardly appears in Greco-Roman letters of those days. It is absent in the literary letters of Cicero and Pliny, and it is rather rare in popular papyrus letters preserved in the parched sands of the Egyptian desert.[2] Only occasionally, when a young migrant writes home to his pious mother, he will add: "Daily I pray for you to God Serapis."[3] Jewish letters show greater piety, at least in a formal way. They often begin with a blessing formula "Blessing of YHWH" or "May YHWH give you to hear words of peace."[4] However these stereotyped formulas cannot compare with the Apostle's lively spontaneity and affectionate identification with the community. With him, prayer flows from his heart, from his faith and his attachment to God's people. Through prayer, he lays before God his "anxiety for all the churches" (2 Cor. 11:28). As he is about to contact them, he joins them in prayer. Closely attuned to the life of these

---

2. A number of those letters can be found in A. Deissmann, *Light from the Ancient East: The New Testament Illustrated by Recently Discovered Texts of the Greco-Roman World* (London: Hodder and Stoughton, 1911), 146–250; C. K. Barrett, *The New Testament Background* (London: SPCK, 1956), 22–47. Cf. J. L. White, ed., "Studies in Ancient Letter Writing," *Semeia* 22 (1982); J. L. White, *Light from Ancient Letters* (Philadelphia: Fortress, 1986); J. L. White, "Ancient Greek Letters," in *Greco-Roman Literature and the New Testament* (SBLSBS 21; ed. D. E. Aune; Atlanta: Scholars Press, 1998).

3. Deissmann, *Light from the Ancient East*, 187–91. See also 180, 184, 187, 194.

4. Cf. D. Pardeee, *Handbook of Ancient Hebrew Letters* (SBLSBS 15; Chico, CA: Scholars Press, 1982), 64–106; A. Lemaire, *Inscriptions hébraïques, I. Les ostraca* (Paris: Cerf, 1977); J. A. Fitzmyer, "Aramaic Epistolography," *Semeia* 22 (1981): 25–57.

communities, his prayer is vibrant and expresses his commitment. It is a prayer that will help the gathering to grow into an *ekklēsia*. There is even good ground to think that this union in prayer had a liturgical background. The letters were read during the celebration of the cult. Through letter and prayer, the Apostle joined in the community meeting. Through prayer, he was affectively and effectively present amid the faithful gathered in celebration.

> Since Paul wrote in his capacity as an apostle of Jesus Christ, his letters were always religious. Consequently, when Paul addressed his congregations, he imagined them at worship and himself as officiating at the service. It is for this reason that he combines epistolary conventions with the language of thanksgiving, blessing, and prayer and why salutation is enjoined as a religious act (e.g., the holy kiss).[5]

Thanksgiving

According to circumstances, this union in prayer will take different forms. Thanksgiving is particularly frequent. Paul sets the tone in 1 Thessalonians, the very first letter that he wrote. From the outset, evangelizing in Europe had yielded encouraging results. In spite of opposition, the first Greeks whom the Apostle had addressed had "received the word in much affliction but with the joy of the Holy Spirit" (1 Thess. 1:6). They stand as a model not only in Greece but "everywhere" (v. 8). These words of encouragement are not mere congratulations, and still less expression of self-satisfaction. The thought turns immediately toward God: "We give thanks to God always for all of you constantly mentioning you in our prayers" (v. 2). This will be a recurring feature in all the letters, even in the short note to Philemon, with the exception of Galatians and 2 Corinthians, to which we shall return.

Thanksgiving is a form of prayer that is found frequently in the Psalms and also in the Gospels (Luke 1:46–56, 68–79; 10:21–22;

---

5. White, "Ancient Greek Letters," 98.

Matt. 11:25–26). It gives the reasons for which we must be grateful to God. As regards the Thessalonians, the reason is their attitude of active faith, generous love, and steadfast hope (1 Thess. 1:3). Yet causes of discouragement were not lacking, and the situation did not incline to optimism. The Word has been received "in much affliction" (1 Thess. 1:6). The new Christians met with a two-sided opposition. On the one hand, their fellow countrymen (1 Thess. 2:14) were disturbed by the growth of what they considered as another branch of Judaism; it was all the more disturbing since it added the attractiveness of not imposing circumcision. Consequently, it did appeal not only to a small ethnic group, the strange practices of which could be overlooked. It was now the entire population that could be tempted to turn away from the imperial cult and the cult of the local gods. On the other hand, the Jews feared a loss of identity if they accepted a faction that claimed to issue from their traditions yet spurned circumcision and the Law (1 Thess. 2:14–16). The situation became so alarming that the Apostle sent his companion Timothy "for fear that somehow the Tempter had brought his work to naught" (1 Thess. 3:5).

In such an anguished situation, a prayer of distress would be expected. Many psalms do it. Similarly, even the early Jerusalem community, evoking Psalm 2, denounces the "raging of the nations" and "the plotting of the nations and of the people of Israel" (Acts 4:24–30). But Paul's prayer does not go that way. Looking up at God, he joyfully admires the wonders of the divine work (1 Thess. 1:6; 2:19–20; 3:9). Psychologists might speak of a positive attitude before existential problems. But the source of Pauline optimism is deeper. It rises from his faith, from a way to look at trials in full confidence in "the God and Father of Our Lord Jesus Christ" (Rom. 15:6; 2 Cor. 1:3; 11:31). "If God is for us, who can be against us? He who did not spare his own Son but gave him up for us all, how will he not also with him graciously give us all things? . . . Who shall separate us from the love of Christ?" (Rom. 8:31–32, 35).

The letter to the Philippians begins also with joy and thanksgiving. There also the situation was far from blissful. Paul was attacked from all sides. Local authorities had jailed him as a troublemaker (Phil. 1:20–24). The accusation was serious; it could lead to the death penalty. Within the community, his authority was challenged by jealous rivals (Phil. 1:15–16). Yet joy remains the keynote of the entire letter (Phil. 1:18, 25; 2:2, 17–18, 28–29; 3:1; 4:1).

The Corinthians gave Paul less cause for satisfaction than the Macedonians of Philippi and Thessalonica. The situation prevailing in that community hardly justified the thanksgiving that opens the first letter addressed to it. The entire letter is a long reproof. The little group that constituted "the church of God that is in Corinth" (1 Cor. 1:2) had just accepted the gospel but seemed to have gotten off to a bad start. The tiny community was already divided in splinter groups which claimed belonging to one or the other of those who had evangelized them (chaps. 1–4). Incest was tolerated (1 Cor. 5:1–2). Their quarrels dragged them to civil court (1 Cor. 6:1–11). Christian freedom was mistaken as sexual licentiousness or, on the opposite, marriage was banned (1 Cor. 7:1–40). Divisions reached even the cooking pot. Was it forbidden to eat meat on the suspicion that what butchers offered might have come from animal offerings in pagan temples? Or, on the contrary, could they turn a blind eye on the possible origin of that stuff? (1 Cor. 8–9). Meals during which the Lord's Supper was commemorated had become opportunities to display social divide (1 Cor. 11:7–31). Prayer meetings turned into pandemonium (1 Cor. 12–14), and finally, to top it all, faith in the Resurrection was itself questioned (1 Cor. 15). Yet Paul says:

> I give thanks to my God always for you because of the grace of God that was given you in Christ Jesus, that in every way you were enriched in him in all speech and all knowledge . . . so that you are not lacking in any spiritual gift, as you wait for the revealing of our Lord Jesus Christ. (1 Cor. 1:4–7)

It has been suggested that there was a touch of irony in this reference to a "knowledge" that pertained more to the Greek thirst for

science and wisdom than to "the knowledge of Jesus Christ and
him crucified" (1 Cor. 2:2). The opening prayer itself would have
mocked the ridiculous self-conceit of these new converts who
boasted of their "knowledge" and the rich gifts of the Spirit. This
interpretation is unlikely; prayer does not lend itself to irony.
Paul is truly in a prayer attitude. In prayer, he places the community before God and reminds it that everything comes from
God through Jesus Christ (v. 4). Later on, he will have to reprove
the Corinthians for having distorted the gifts of God and made it
a matter of vainglory. But the initial step will be to contemplate
the divine work and invite the Corinthians to join him in prayer
before God in the midst of their problems.

Intercession

Thanksgiving turned the eyes toward God. Intercession will pray
God to turn his eyes to the human condition. The psalter presents
many examples of this type of prayer. In the Gospels, a typical
illustration is the great intercessory prayer of Jesus in John 17. In
Pauline epistles also, this form of prayer follows frequently the
initial thanksgiving.

Thus, in 1 Thessalonians, after having rendered thanks for the
cause of joy found in the faithfulness of the community (1 Thess.
3:8), Paul goes on to say: "We pray most earnestly night and day
that we may see you face to face and supply what is lacking in
your faith . . . and may the Lord make you increase and abound
in love for one another and for all, as we do for you, so that he
may establish your hearts blameless in holiness before our God
and Father, at the coming of our Lord Jesus with all his saints"
(1 Thess. 3:10, 12–13). In the same way, in Philippians 1:9–11, the
thanksgiving turns into intercession: "And it is my prayer that
your love may abound more and more, with knowledge and all
discernment, so that you may approve what is excellent, and so
be pure and blameless for the day of Christ, filled with the fruit
of righteousness that comes through Jesus Christ, to the glory
and praise of God." The initial prayer of Romans is also made of
two parts: thanksgiving (Rom. 1:8–9) and the prayer of petition,

for himself that his intended journey may succeed (v. 10), and for the community that it may be strengthened (v. 11). What this "strengthening" implies will be specified in the concluding prayer: "May the God of endurance and encouragement grant you to live in such harmony with one another, in accord with Christ Jesus. . . . May the God of hope fill you with all joy and peace in believing, so that by the power of the Holy Spirit you may abound in hope" (Rom. 15:5, 13).

The object of the prayer is noteworthy. In a context of opposition and hostility, when life itself is in danger, we would expect a prayer asking for protection against those perils and for help to thwart those attacks. But Paul does not ask, for himself and the community, to be freed from enemies. On the contrary, in the midst of adversities, he can say: "In that I rejoice. Yes, and I will rejoice, for I know that through your prayers and the help of the Spirit of Jesus Christ this will turn out for my deliverance" (Phil. 1:18–19). He is about to stand in trial, but the outcome leaves him indifferent, "as it is my eager expectation and hope that I will not be at all ashamed, but that with full courage now as always Christ will be honored in my body, whether by life or by death. For to me to live is Christ, and to die is gain" (Phil. 1:20–21). He does not pray for himself but for the community, and what he asks for is its strengthening in holiness, growth in faith (Rom. 1:12) and love (1 Thess. 3:12–13; Phil. 1:9) and fullness of "joy and peace in faith abounding in hope by the power of the Holy Spirit" (Rom. 15:13). The main issue does not come from outside; "weaknesses, insults, hardships, persecutions and calamities for Christ" are only opportunities to unveil "the power of Christ" (2 Cor. 11:10). Intercessory prayer intends mainly to turn to this "power of Christ" so that the community may answer better and better to the call and grace of the new covenant.

Hymn

The Corinthians caused much worry to their Apostle. A first letter did not suffice to set things right. A second letter had to follow.

"No other letter of Paul evokes so vividly the image of a suffering and rejected apostle, misunderstood by his fellow Christians."[6]

This may be the reason why 2 Corinthians does not begin with the usual thanksgiving. The situation is so bad that it moves Paul to tears (2 Cor. 2:4). He has nothing to rejoice about and no reason to sing in thanksgiving. God only is left; the Apostle can only turn to him. Thanksgiving and intercession stemmed out of the concrete situation and entered into dialogue between God and human condition. In the hymn, the distressed Apostle is left with God alone. Whatever may be the situation, when everything seems to be lost, God remains, and God is "the God and Father of our Lord Jesus Christ, the Father of mercies and God of all comfort who comforts us in all our affliction so that we may be able to comfort those who are in any affliction with the comfort with which we are ourselves are comforted by God" (2 Cor. 1:3–4). Everything could lead to discouragement; as Paul puts it, on account "of the affliction we experienced in Asia, we were so utterly burdened beyond our strength that we despaired of life itself. Indeed, we felt that we had received the sentence of death" (2 Cor. 1:8–9). There remains only the confidence based, not on any human resource, but "on God who raises the dead" (2 Cor. 1:9). Paul looks at his trials in the light of Christ; "as we share abundantly in Christ's sufferings, so through Christ we share abundantly in comfort too" (2 Cor. 1:5). Finally having found peace in this recourse to the power of the Resurrection, Paul can revive the dialogue with the community, and the opening prayer ends with a call to cooperate in prayer: "You also must help us by prayer, so that many will give thanks on our behalf for the blessing granted us through the prayers of many" (2 Cor. 1:11).

The letter to the Galatians is the only one that has no introductory prayer. A kind of hymn can be seen in the dry liturgical formula of Galatians 1:5: "to him be glory for ever and ever." But immediately the Apostle expresses his disappointment with

---

6. R. E. Brown, *Introduction to the New Testament* (2nd ed.; New York: Doubleday, 2009), 541.

the Galatians who, hardly evangelized, have turned to "another gospel" (Gal. 1:6). He does not mince words: "I am astonished" at your attitude (Gal. 1:6). "Stupid Galatians!" (Gal. 3:1), he exclaims. His indignation leads him close to coarseness; if the opponents advocate circumcision, they could as well cut it all! (Gal. 5:12). In conclusion, he writes in his own hand and in bold letters; "from now on, let no one cause me trouble, for I bear on my body the marks of Jesus" (Gal. 6:17). However, he concludes with a double blessing: "Peace and mercy" (Gal. 6:16). "The grace of our Lord Jesus Christ be with your spirit, brothers" (Gal. 6:18). He borrows the ritual formula that concludes the epistles, but he adds the word "Brothers!" This will be the departing word of the letter; it brings "an affectionate addendum"[7] to the concluding formula. Earlier, his sorrow had been expressed in terms of affectionate fondness. It was the sufferings of a mother in birth pangs (Gal. 4:19). Whatever might have been the misunderstandings, he remains united with the Galatians by bonds of love. Paul is emotive. He is so in the expression of his disappointments as well as of his attachments. This brings him quite close to our human weaknesses and mood swings. The letter to the Galatians is the work of a great thinker. It is also the voice of a bewildered father looking at his wayward children. But always he looks up to God.

Contemplation

We must also and above all consider a form of Pauline prayer that does not belong to any of the classical genres of thanksgiving, intercession, and hymn. It is the prayer in which Paul, filled with wonder and bewildered, contemplates "the mystery that was kept secret for long ages but has now been disclosed and through the prophetic writings has been made known to all nations, according to the command of the eternal God, to bring about the obedience of faith" (Rom. 16:25–26). In this contemplation, the bond of love that unites the Apostle with the "Father of Our Lord Jesus Christ"

---

7. S. Légasse, *L'épître de Paul aux Galates* (LDCom 9; Paris: Cerf, 2000), 487.

finds its strongest expression. This contemplation concludes also the first part of the letter to the Romans in 8:31–39. The previous chapters had shown how "where sin increased, grace abounded all the more, so that, as sin reigned in death, grace also might reign through righteousness leading to eternal life through Jesus Christ our Lord" (Rom. 5:20–21). He concludes: "What else can we say?" There is nothing left to expound. Only contemplation is left before the God who did not spare his own Son who, by his death and Resurrection, has manifested "the love of God revealed in Jesus Christ our Lord." Translations entitle the passage "hymn to the love of God." The theme is well perceived. Paul speaks of the love of God for humanity.[8] But the qualification of the passage as a hymn would be inadequate. A hymn is language addressed to God as in the beginning of 2 Corinthians. In Romans 8 and 16, Paul does not speak to God to praise him. He gazes and contemplates.

The "hymn to Christ" of Philippians 2:6–11 can also be considered as contemplation. Here also the so-called "hymn" is not addressed to Christ as a hymn would be. It is a contemplative look cast at Christ in his abasement and his exaltation. This is not the place to go into the many problems of interpretation raised by the text. These problems reflect only the mysterious tone of a mystical contemplation.

The Praise of Love in 1 Corinthians 13 is also a form of contemplation. It hardly looks like a prayer since it is not addressed to God or to Christ and makes no mention of the Spirit. Should it therefore be considered as a profane eulogy as the odes to the Fatherland, Victory, or Liberty? But Paul is no Pindar or Horace. He is a man of faith, haunted by Christ (2 Cor. 5:14). As seen above, his Christian faith underlies his eulogy of *agapē*.

Wisdom, Spirit of God, Love, *kenosis*, Cross: the Pauline thought is always turned toward the same luminous

---

8. And not of the love of men for God as some editions of the NAB would have it.

and victorious horizon. . . . In Jesus, Paul contemplates a plenitude, a liberty, a Wisdom, a Spirit, a supreme Good, a Love which alone matters and which can do everything. His whole approach . . . consists in bringing out forcefully this wonderful presence that is beyond any human effort or achievement.[9]

As in the Ode of Romans 8, the "I" or the "we" of Christian identity contemplates divine love. But, whereas in Romans, the Christian "I" turns toward Christ and divine love manifested in Christ, in 1 Corinthians 13, it considers the way in which this love affects human existence. Anyway in both 1 Corinthians 13 and Romans 8:39, it is the mystery of "the love of God manifested in Jesus Christ our Lord" (Rom. 8:39) that is contemplated.

The Invocation

"Everyone who invokes the name of the Lord will be saved." How then will they call on him in whom they have not believed? And how are they to believe in him of whom they have never heard? And how are they to hear without someone preaching? (Rom. 10:13–14)

In this text, which analyses the stages of the mission, the final significance of "invocation" will be noted. In the process that leads to salvation, faith is not the ultimate stage. Faith leads to invocation. Faith is not only mental assent; it must also be a cry from the heart, arising from the depth of one's soul.

Invocation is prayer as a cry. It can be a cry of distress like the cry of the disciples in the storm (Matt. 8:25), like the *kyrie eleison*, the Christian SOS. It can be also a battle cry or a cry of victory like the *teruah* of the wars of Yahweh,[10] or the triumphal cries

---

9. B. Standaert, *Le ministère de Paul: Parole, prière, miséricorde* (Paris: Mediaspaul, 2016), 141.

10. "The *teruah* was originally a wild acclamation meant to stir the fighters and to discourage the enemies. But it was also a religious cry, connected with the role of the Ark of the Covenant in battles (cf. 1 Sam. 4:5f.).

of Revelation 7:10, 12; 11:15; 19:1, 5, 16. Also, and mostly, the invocation can be a cry of love, like the "Mummy!" of the child and the amorous calls of the Song of Songs. The invocation is characterized by its brevity, since the cry from the heart is not discursive, and by the intensity of the emotive power that it carries.[11]

Pauline letters report two main invocations of the early church: "Jesus is the Lord!" and "Abba! Father." They have a high significance since they condense in two outcries the essential attitude of the believer toward Christ and toward God.

"Jesus is the Lord!" is the triumphal conclusion of the christological hymn of Philippians 2:6–11. The hymn is likely to be anterior to Paul, and the concluding shout of triumph is itself anterior to the hymn. It represents a most ancient form of faith confession in the lordship of Jesus Christ. The original context may be found in 1 Corinthians 12:3; it evokes the early prayer meetings when, in a charismatic style, faith was enthusiastically proclaimed. In the Greek text of Philippians 2:11, as in 1 Corinthians 12:3, the word "Lord" comes first to give it greater emphasis: "Lord is Jesus Christ." It is the triumphal shout of victory of Life over Death. Through his Resurrection, the Crucified One has acquired universal lordship and put all the evil powers under his feet (cf. 1 Cor. 15:25–27). This proclamation of Jesus's lordship was also a challenge to the Roman Caesar and his claim to be the universal and absolute *kyrios*. This cry was also the confession of faith accompanying Baptism (Rom. 10:8). It contained the sum total of faith in Christ and trust in the power of his Resurrection.

The other invocation is the love cry "Abba! Father." It summarizes in a single word the faith inherited from Jesus. It was Jesus's prayer. It was still his cry of anguished love at Gethsemane when

---

It became part of the ritual of the Ark (2 Sam. 6:15) and finally of the Temple ritual (Lev. 23:24; Num. 29:1 and Pss. *passim*)" (R. de Vaux, *Les institutions de l'Ancien Testament* [Paris: Cerf, 1969], 2:67).

11. We may think of the Islamic shout *Allah hu akbar* or, better, of the *Ram! Ram!* on the lips of expiring Mahatma Gandhi, or again of the cry of *Jesus: Jesus!* of Joan of Arc at the stake.

love reached its full sacrificial depth and, when saying "Abba!" meant also "Thy will be done." He taught this prayer to his disciples (Luke 11:2–4; Matt. 6:9–13). He taught them also its meaning: "All things have been handed over to me by my Father, and no one knows the Son except the Father, and no one knows the Father except the Son and anyone to whom the Son chooses to reveal him" (Matt. 11:27). The Son knows the Father. He lives in a relationship of moving intimacy with the God of love. He "reveals" this knowledge; such is the Good News he brings to the world. It was his mission, and it will be the mission of the disciples. The mission of the church issues from this cry of love: "Abba! Father."

The early church received this message and this invocation. Accepting the Good News means joining in the love cry of Jesus. It was so impressive that even the Hellenistic communities retained it in its original Aramaic form. To the Galatians tempted to depart from the gospel, Paul recalls their outcry[12] in prayer: "Because you are sons, God sent the Spirit of his Son into our hearts, crying: 'Abba! Father!'" (Gal. 4:6). The turn of the sentence is paradoxical; it seems as though the Spirit himself were praying the Father. The parallel text of Romans 8:14–16 has rectified the formulation and developed the idea: "For all who are led by the Spirit of God are sons of God. For you did not receive the spirit of slavery to fall back into fear, but you have received the Spirit of adoption as sons, by whom we cry, 'Abba! Father!' The Spirit himself bears witness with our spirit that we are children of God" (Rom. 8:14–16).

The burning cry of love addressed to the "God and Father of our Lord Jesus Christ" (Rom. 15:6) is no mere human word: it is the Spirit of the Son sent by the Father who inspires in the

---

12. The text of both Romans and Galatians has the Greek verb *krazein,* which means "shouting." "We need not understand in the sense of shouting and clamoring. Cf. the "groaning" in Rom. 8:23" (Légasse, *L'épître de Paul aux Romains*, 514). It is at least the expression of an "ardent prayer" shared loudly in liturgical gatherings.

believer the sense of filial intimacy that inspired Jesus himself. Christian prayer merges into the fundamental "knowledge" of the Father that the Son had. The mission stems from this revelation that comes from the Son.

Conclusion

Paul recommends persevering in prayer (Rom. 12:12; cf. 1 Thess. 5:17–18, 25; 1 Cor. 7:5; Phil. 4:6). But he does not say whether he trained his neophytes in prayer and how he did it. He did not write an *Introduction to the Devout Life*. Neither do we know how he prayed when making his way, walking, or traveling at the slow rate of a heavy chariot. Or again, how did he turn to God at night, in the lodgings at the end of a long journey or of a hard-working day? Imprisonment gave him ample time to pray, and Luke reports the prayer of the prisoner (Acts 16:25; 23:11; 27:24, 35). But Paul himself makes no mention of it. We shall not know how he prayed "most earnestly night and day" that he might again see the Christians of Thessalonica and supply what was still lacking in their faith (1 Thess. 3:10). Still less does he linger over the ecstasy that caught him up to the third heaven into paradise. He hides his identity and concludes that these experiences were "things that cannot be told, which man may not enter" (2 Cor. 12:2–4). This part of his personal prayer life remains hidden. Given his familiarity with the Scriptures, they must have fed his prayer. But he keeps silent about it.

Therefore, a systematic treatise on oration will not be found in his letters. Since it was a correspondence relating to his missionary task, it referred to prayer from that angle. However, his mission was the heart of his life, and consequently his apostolic prayer reaches the depth of his soul. With Paul, prayer goes along with action and action with prayer. Prayer stems from action. Action is nourished by prayer and goes to the innermost center of any prayer, "the Spirit of sonship by whom we cry: 'Abba! Father!'" There is the focus where prayer and apostolic action converge. It is not quite accurate to say that prayer is the soul of Paul's apostolate. The link between prayer and action goes deeper. The soul of both prayer and apostolate is the Spirit that "comes to the help of our weakness" and, even if "we do not know what to pray for or as we ought . . . himself intercedes for us with groanings too deep for words" (Rom. 8:26).

So, mission and prayer are not only intertwined. They merge together in a fundamental identity. The service of the gospel constitutes the cult of the new covenant in the Spirit. In the beginning of the letter to the Romans, the Apostle introduced himself as the one who "worshiped with [his] spirit by preaching the Gospel of his Son" (Rom. 1:9).[13] The text is so concise as to be obscure. The end of the letter will be clearer:

> On some points I have written to you very boldly by way of reminder, because of the grace given me by God to be a minister[14] of Christ Jesus to the Gentiles in the priestly service[15] of the gospel of God, so that the offering of the Gentiles may be acceptable, sanctified by the Holy Spirit. (Rom. 15:15–16)[16]

---

13. NJB translation. The text could be understood of a ministry of prayer that would accompany the ministry of the Gospel as in Acts 6:4. Rather it identifies the proclamation of the Good News with the cult (*latreia*), as shown in the parallel text of 15:16: the proclamation of the Good News *is* the spiritual cult.

14. The Greek word for "minister" here is *leitourgos*, which evokes "liturgical" function. By itself, the word may have other connotations than the cultic one. But the immediate context specifies that the work of the *leitourgos* consists in *hierourgounta*, a priestly service. Cf. C. Spicq, art. *leitourgos, TLNT*, 386.

15. The Greek word is *hierourgounta*, which combines the roots *hiero-* (sacred) and *erg-* (work, function).

16. For a more elaborate study of the text, in addition to the commentaries, see A. M. Denis, "La fonction apostolique et la liturgie nouvelle. Étude thématique des métaphores pauliniennes du culte nouveau," *RSPT* 42 (1958): 403–8; J. Ponthot, "L'expression cultuelle du ministère paulinien selon Rom 15,26," in *L'apôtre Paul* (BETL 73; ed. A. Vanhoye; Leuven: University Press, 1986), 254–62; C. Tassin, *L'apôtre Paul: Un autoprotrait* (Paris: Desclée de Brouwer, 2009), 180–90.

"The offering of the Gentiles sanctified by the Holy Spirit" is the "obedience of faith," as in Romans 1:5 and 16:26, the entire commitment of oneself in response to the Good News. So also, in Romans 12:1, the life of the believer was compared to a sacrificial offering. "I appeal to you therefore, brothers, by the mercies of God, to present your bodies as a living sacrifice, holy and acceptable to God, which is your spiritual worship."[17] This "spiritual worship" had already been announced by the prophets. It is "the broken spirit, the broken and contrite heart," as opposed to the "burnt offerings and whole burnt sacrifices" (Ps. 51:18–19). "I desire steadfast love and not sacrifice, the knowledge of God rather than burnt offerings," said God through the prophet Hosea (Hos. 6:6; cf. Isa. 1:10–20; Amos 5:21–24). Such is the cult of the new covenant offered in the temple of the Holy Spirit, which the believing community constitutes (1 Cor. 3:16), and even the body of every believer united to the body of Christ (1 Cor. 6:19).

The apostle, minister of the gospel, who led the nations to "the obedience of faith," fulfills the "sacred function" of the priest taking the spiritual offering to the temple of the Spirit.

The apostle is a *leitourgos* because he functions as a priest (*hierourgounta*) through the proclamation of the Gospel, offering thereby to God an acceptable offering, i.e. the nations converted by the Holy Spirit. . . . Therefore, he who announces the Good News assumes a sacerdotal function, as the priest of old in the Temple offered animal victims. Just like the priest, the apostle fulfills the mission of preparing the return of men to God through the offering of a sacrificial victim.[18]

---

17. In "*spiritual* worship," the Greek word is *logikon*, that is, belonging to the order of the *logos*, of the order transcending the material level.

18. F. J. Leenhardt, *L'épître de Saint Paul aux Romains* (CNT 6; Neuchâtel: Delachaux & Niestlé, 1957), 207.

There is no dichotomy between prayer and mission. The cult of the new covenant is the self-offering in the obedience of faith. Bringing the gospel to the world, the Apostle prepares this "living sacrifice, holy and acceptable to God" (Rom. 11:1) and celebrates the cult of the universal temple open to all the nations.

Conclusion

We may now return to the question raised in the Preface. Was Paul a missionary? Is he the model of missionaries? He is certainly so for Luke, in the Acts of the Apostles. Luke has described a wayfaring Paul, going from town to town, proclaiming the Good News to the Gentiles, pushed by the Spirit to go ever farther. On the way, with great zeal and courage, he faces many obstacles, meets with unexpected successes and equally unexpected failures. He is jailed, narrowly escapes scourging, and is the victim of a shipwreck. Finally, he reaches Rome as a captive. The book seems to be left unfinished. We do not know what happened subsequently. The reader is left with the image of Paul under house arrest, yet "proclaiming the Kingdom of God and teaching about the Lord Jesus Christ with all boldness and without hindrance" (Acts 28:31). The program outlined in Acts 1:8 has not been completed. Rome is not the "end of the earth." It is rather the center of the pagan world. So, Luke leaves it to the readers to continue the mission and, in course of time, to take it to "the end of the world." As it was for Paul, their mission will meet with many trials, but the word of God cannot be shackled.

If Luke deserves to be blamed, it is for having been too successful. The portrait that he has drawn has caught Christian imagination and has even predominated in the canon of the New Testament. There has not been any other similar artist to depict what could have been the mission of Matthew, of John, and even possibly of James. As described by Luke, the Pauline mission has established itself as the prototypical mission, and even tended to be considered as the only mission. Yet Paul did not claim monopoly over the mission. He knew of other types of mission and recognized them. He did not consider himself as the only apostle, as if he had been *the* apostle, in haughty isolation facing a timorous apostolic group, fearfully trapped in a shortsighted vision limited to Palestinian Judaism. This would be a misunderstanding of the allotment of responsibilities decided at the Jerusalem Assembly, which recognized the authenticity and even the priority of the ministry to the "circumcision" (Gal. 2:8–9).

However, the Pauline model of mission presented by Luke should not be misunderstood. It cannot be reduced to the image of the missionary rushing headlong all over the world. The Lukan image of Paul is not lacking in depth. Paul's journeys follow the dynamics of Jesus's journey toward the city where the divine plan shall be accomplished (Luke 9:51). The Pauline moves are not mere human projects. They are led by the Spirit, the true protagonist of the venture. Paul is carried by the Word more than he carries it. The final stage will take place in the context of a captivity, as a kind of Passion. Like the journey of Jesus, the way of Paul in Acts has paschal overtones.

Yet the main difference that Luke brings to the original picture consists precisely in that, in the Acts, he presented his hero as a model for a mission, expected to be carried on beyond Rome and after Paul. Luke wrote his account some thirty years after the events that he relates. With the hindsight of all these years, he sees Paul as a paradigm of the ensuing mission.

If, for Luke, Paul was a mission model, Paul himself takes us rather to the original source of the mission, to the founding event of the Resurrection of Jesus crucified. In the Resurrection of Jesus Christ, Paul has perceived the dawn of the new times. "Behold, now is the favorable time; behold now is the day of salvation" (2 Cor. 6:2). He will have to realize gradually that the "day" has to extend over time. However, the focus remains Jesus's Resurrection, perceived as the primordial burst of light, life, and power and as the outbreak of a new world. For Paul, it was the "illumination of the Good News of the glory of Christ, who is the image of God" (2 Cor. 4:4). His role will be to "to give the light of the knowledge of the glory of God in the face of Jesus Christ" (2 Cor. 4:6). The entire mission of the Apostle stems from this illumination and is marked by it.

Beyond the individual communication of the Good News of the Risen Lord, Paul's vision assumes all the dimensions of the significance of the Resurrection. It is perceived in line with the Jewish perspective of the People of God, People of the Promises and of the Covenant. Prophets had announced that the last days would see a new covenant in the Spirit, open to the nations. Ezekiel had described the final resurrection (Ezek. 37) and the gift of a new heart and of a new spirit (Ezek. 36:26; cf. Ps. 51:12). Jesus's Resurrection means that these days have come, that the promises have been accomplished, and that God will now establish the People of the New Covenant—the covenant according to the Spirit which is no longer defined by the Law but by faith in what Jesus Christ signifies. God intends to give his people this deepened identity, and this enlarged extension to the nations.

Therefore, the mission approach of Paul is not limited to a "propagation of faith" that would concern only individual adepts. His project is collective. It embraces all the dimensions of the life of a people. It has also the depth of the life of a people belonging to God, sharing in his holiness, and living of his love. Minister of the New Covenant according to the Spirit, Paul will set up *ekklēsiai*, communities of the new covenant, transformed by the Spirit, living of faith in the Risen One, united in love, first fruits of the eschatological gathering of the People of God.

Sent to the nations, he comes out of the Jewish Diaspora where he could have felt at home and gives himself to the world of the nations. He goes over to the fringes, not only to the geographical outskirts like Rome and even Spain, but also to the ethnic, social, and cultural foreign spheres. He could have comfortably remained within his Diaspora milieu; he accepts to move out of his familiar landmarks and becomes "all to all" (1 Cor. 9:22). The "power of the Resurrection" breaks natural solidarities based on nation, clan, class, and ethnic bonds and creates a new brotherhood knitted together by "faith active in love" (Gal. 5:6).

Paul made a long journey on the roads of the Roman Empire, but his internal journey of ethnic dispossession and transcultural uprooting is still more significant. It was the way that the Galilean Good News had to follow to become the universal gospel message of salvation to all the nations.

A spiritual process underlay this apostolic development. It can be compared to the ways of spiritual growth in Christian mysticism. At the same time as Paul moved toward the fringes, he deepened internally the fundamental experience of his encounter with the Risen One in whom he perceived "the illumination of the Good News of the glory of Christ, who is the image of God" (2 Cor. 4:4). This "image of God" is recognized "on the face of Jesus Christ," luminous source irradiating "the light of the knowledge of the glory of God" (2 Cor. 4:6).

The "face of Christ" is the defiled and tortured visage of the Crucified One who abased and emptied himself, taking the form of a slave, to the point of death, even death on a cross (Phil. 2:7–8). It is on that face that is manifested the love of God the Father who, by giving up his Son for us all, has thereby given us all things (Rom. 8:32). On this face, Paul reads the demonstration of the love of God: "God proves his love for us in that while we were still sinners, Christ died for us" (Rom. 5:8).

The "face of Christ" is also the visage of the Risen One. The Resurrection reveals the power of this divine love, power of life and of new creation, mightier than any earthly and heavenly power, stronger than death itself, triumph of life over forces of destruction (Rom. 8:37–38). The face of the Crucified and Risen One is the ultimate expression of the glory of God, ultimate theophany, more dazzling than the Sinai lightnings. The contemplation of "the face of Christ" reaches "even the depths of God" (1 Cor. 2:10), the mysteries of a wisdom and of a power that shatter the forces and values of the world (1 Cor. 1:22–25). The mission will be nourished by this contemplation. It will irradiate the nations, the People of the New Covenant, with the splendor of the glory of God on the face of Christ. It will allow them to take part, through faith, in the encounter with the Risen One, first fruits of the new life in the Spirit and dawn of the new world.

By making Paul the model of the missionary, Luke normalized the Pauline mission, aligning it with the typology of the itinerant missionary. By allowing us to share in his foundational experience, Paul takes us to the vital essence of the mission. Like the Apostle, "working together with God" (2 Cor. 6:1), the mission gathers God's people in communities of faith and love, witnesses to the advent of a new world. The "mind of Christ" (1 Cor. 2:16), the "conformity" (Phil. 3:10) with what Christ signifies, will be the soul of this mission. The "power of the Resurrection" will be its force.

Index of Passages

Scripture Passages

12:29	100	2:47	124	13:5	97
14:12	93	4:4	63, 85	13:7	63
14:14	93	4:24–30	181	13:8–13	142
16:15	127	4:29	63	13:9	169
		4:31	63	13:14–43	117
Luke		4:32	126	13:43	83
1:35	170	4:36–37	149	13:44–52	149
1:46–56	180	5:11	81	13:48	63
1:68–79	180	5:14	85	13:52	169
2:32	89	5:34–39	11	14:1	117
4:18–19	57	6:1–7	85	14:4	29n3
4:18	56	6:4	192n13	14:8–10	142
4:38	175n3	6:7	63	15:1–4	149
8:37	175n3	6:13	29	15:4	81
9:10	29n2	8:1–40	134	15:7	62, 63
9:51	133, 196	8:13	81	15:8–9	169
10:21–22	180	8:16	91	15:21	120, 121
11:2–4	190	8:25	63	15:22	81
24:48	126	8:36–38	91	15:28	169
		9:1–19	25	15:36	97
John		9:1	12	15:37–40	150
1:1	100	9:3	25, 149	16:5	85
17	183	9:4	25	16:6–9	170
17:21–23	126	9:5	25	16:13	117
20:21–23	127	9:10–19	26	16:14–15	138
		9:10	29	16:15	91
Acts		9:15	1, 25, 26	16:17	44
1:1	61	9:16	26	16:22–24	130
1:7	89	9:26–27	149	16:25–40	142
1:8	126, 134, 195	9:31	85	16:25	191
1:12	85	9:32–11:18	134	16:33	91
1:14–15	123	10	117	16:37	2
1:21–22	29, 40	10:44	63	16:39	131
1:22	26	10:47–48	91	17:1–2	117
1:47	85	11:1	63	17:5	29
2–7	134	11:21	85	17:10	117
2	123	11:22–24	149	17:11	63
2:1–13	170	11:22	81	17:18	73, 87
2:1	123	11:25	149	17:21	73
2:4	123	12:1	81	17:22–23	119
2:9–11	118	12:24	63	17:23	97
2:14–41	124	13	41	18:1–4	117
2:41	85	13:1–3	40, 149, 169	18:1–2	148
2:42–47	126	13:2	41	18:3–4	138
2:42	91	13:5–6	117	18:3	9, 131, 138

Other Writings